The Author / Kenneth O. Gangel is Professor and Chairman of the Department of Christian Education at Dallas Theological Seminary. He is a graduate of Taylor University, Grace Theological Seminary, and Concordia Seminary. Dr. Gangel received his Ph.D. in college administration from the University of Missouri. He has written many articles and books, including *Unwrap Your Spiritual Gifts* and *The Church Education Handbook*, both from Victor Books. Dr. Gangel is married and the father of two children.

24 Ways to

IMPROVE
your
TEACHING

Kenneth O. Gangel

VICTOR BOOKS™
A DIVISION OF SCRIPTURE PRESS PUBLICATIONS INC.
USA CANADA ENGLAND

The contents of this book originally appeared
as a series of articles in
The Sunday School Times and Gospel Herald,
and is adapted with permission of Union Gospel Press,
Cleveland, Ohio.

Bible quotations are from the *King James Version* unless otherwise identified. Also quoted is the *New American Standard Bible* (NASB), © the
Lockman Foundation 1960, 1962, 1963, 1968, 1971, 1972, 1973, 1975,
1977. Used by permission.

Twelfth printing, 1986

Library of Congress Catalog Card Number: 74-77453
ISBN: 0-89693-235-4

© 1974 by SP Publications, Inc.

Contents

Thinking about Teaching Methods

John Wesley was sarcastically dubbed a "methodist" when he began to promote an organized approach to the communication of the Gospel. His commitment to method implies that there is a disorganized way to communicate the truth as well as an organized way. Wesley's success, demonstrated by his place in history, is a strong argument for the latter.

The word *method* is simply descriptive of processes and techniques used by a teacher to communicate information to the students. Because classes differ in interests, mental ability, and attention span, the teacher must use teaching methods which are appropriate for his group. Children have learning characteristics which differ considerably from those of adults, so teaching methods which may be very effective with adults will not necessarily achieve communication with children.

The age of the students, however, is only one of the issues involved in choosing the appropriate teaching method. Another major factor is the *objective of the lesson*. What goals are to be accomplished in the classroom period? Can the goals chosen be achieved best through a large amount of pupil participation, or do they require transmission of a generous portion of content? Apart from the crucial concern for biblical theology, there is nothing more important in preparing to teach than a clarification of objectives.

In 14 years of preparing college and seminary students to be teachers, I have found their major collective hang-up to be clumsy construction of teaching objectives. As Findley Edge has well reminded us, good teaching objectives should be brief enough to be remembered, clear enough to be written down, and specific enough to be achieved (*Teaching for Results,* Broadman Press, Nashville, Tenn.).

More recent emphases focus on the necessity of formulating objectives in terms of *student behavior.* For example, rather than saying, "To help the class realize the importance of daily prayer," one could state the objective like this: "The student will understand the importance of daily prayer and begin a program of daily personal devotions." Such an objective is brief, clear, specific, and describes something that the teacher wishes to happen in the life of the student. When this kind of objective is developed, the road to selection of method can be walked more easily.

A third factor influencing the method selected is the *content of the lesson itself.* A historical lesson from the book of Acts for high schoolers could lend itself well to an illustrated presentation with the use of good Bible maps. On the other hand, the principles of Christian separation expounded by the Apostle Paul in 1 Corinthians 6 would be handled better in that same class through open discussion.

One danger teachers face is the constant temptation to offer excuses for lack of variety in teaching methodology. Many teachers excuse their consistent gravitation to the lecture method by suggesting that the *amount* of content, or perhaps the *nature* of the content, requires that approach. Actually, they are probably guilty of not thinking creatively with regard to methodology.

These three factors are perhaps the most important criteria for the choice of teaching method, but they are by no means the only ones. Additional items include *available resources, educational background of the students,* and, very important, the *time allotment* for the teaching period. The thinking teacher is aware of all of these variables and applies them appropriately in his preparation.

The variety of teaching methods is almost limitless. It may be helpful to think in terms of categories of method. For example, one type of communication emphasizes the teacher as the performer in the educational process. One might call this *teacher-to-student communication.* Within this category such methods as lecture, storytelling, and demonstration would be included. Obviously these methods are primarily monological. They lend themselves to large groups, coverage of much content, and groups of learners who have minimal preparation for the classtime. Usually, teachers with less training and experience tend toward this category since it is easier to use than most others. Unfortunately they form habits which persist years later when they have gained experience worthy of a greater variety in teaching method. As someone has said, the only bad method is one which is *used all of the time.*

A second general category of method might be called *student-to-teacher* communication. This is a monologue in the other direction. The student performs, and the teacher plays a listening role. In this category we would expect to find such methods as recitation, reports, and testing. Obviously such student performance must be planned and motivated by the teacher, but communication is still basically on a one-way track. Here the preparation time for the student is increased. He must know in advance of the class period what is expected of him and how he should utilize preparation time.

Two-way communication between teacher and student is another approach to teaching methodology. In the opinion of many professional educators, this category exceeds the first two in effectiveness. It emphasizes an involvement of both teacher and pupil in the mutual quest for truth. Two different methods must be included here. The method called *question and answer* is distinguished from the method called *discussion* by the kind of questions asked. When teaching by *question and answer,* the teacher either asks or answers objective questions, usually based on some item of a factual nature.

In *discussion,* thought questions are used. These generally lead the class to penetrate the subject with a much higher degree of perception and perspective. The teacher who would teach by *discussion* must spend a considerable amount of time preparing the kind and sequence of questions which he will use. Successful two-way teaching is dependent upon effective preparation by both teacher and student.

Group activities represent yet a different kind of teaching method. A wide range of group activities can be utilized. The emphasis here is on multiple instructional involvement. Panels, debates, buzz groups, and all forms of drama could be included here. The collective planning, preparation, and participation offer a significant contribution to the learning experience of the entire class.

Teachers who work with smaller children would certainly want to include instructive play as a method category. Methods in this list are generally used with children from the earliest years of instruction up through junior age. They include various kinds of games and toys, use of a sand table, puppets, fingerplays, puzzles and contests, action songs, and simple role playing. At one time in the history of education, it was thought that fun and learning were not mutually compatible. Now we know, however, that interest is one of the important keys to learning, and good elementary teaching incorporates as much instructive play as possible.

A final category might be designated nonclassroom activity. In all serious education the teacher is concerned that students prepare themselves for class by studying in advance. Guided preparation, carefully related to class sessions, can contribute much to mental and spiritual growth. Nonclassroom activity, however, refers to anything that happens outside of class providing it is a part of a planned instructional effort. It could happen before a given class session or could take the form of follow-up or carry-through. In this general category consider such methods as field trips, guided research, and various kinds of projects.

The teacher who wishes to be really effective will be sure that his teaching is characterized by variety. In developing variety the teacher must become acquainted with various methods. He must try these and analyze them in use over a period of time. This implies that he must use lesson plans and keep records that enable him to compare various teaching strategies. The teacher's own attitude toward his ministry is very important. If he recognizes teaching as genuine service for Christ which must meet high standards, he may see variety as one of those standards of excellence toward which he must constantly be striving. The conscientious teacher can learn new methods by reading helpful literature, observing effective teachers, and attending workshops and conferences. In the final analysis, however, he will have to experiment, because continual effort and experience are a necessary part of teaching progress.

The methods described in this book are not new. There is no pretense of "different and creative" approaches to teaching (which are too often neither new nor creative). I am concerned that teachers understand the recognized methods, their strengths, limitations, and some principles for their effective use.

1
Learning Through the Lecture

Someone has defined lecture as a process by which information goes from the notes of a teacher to the notes of a student without having gone through the head of either! Such digs are offered only partly in jest. The lecture has suffered in recent years from attacks by critics and lack of response by students, but most of all, from misuse by teachers.

Is any teaching method absolutely *better* than the others? Probably not. The variable factors mentioned in the introduction (if you skipped it, please go back and read it now) make it a relative value choice each time. The lecture method is not inherently bad. Misuse rather than use is the culprit.

Originally, a professor's lectures consisted of reading from the textbooks while the students took copious notes. The term itself comes from the Latin word *legere* ("to read"). Lecturing is simply a process of teaching in which an instructor gives an oral presentation of facts or concepts. The procedure involves the clarification or explanation of some major idea which has been formed into a question or a problem.

The lecture technique has three basic aims. The first and most important is *the communication of information*. With the knowledge explosion of our day, students in any educational situation lack enormous amounts of information. There is relatively little time for them to get it inductively, so an overview of the subject matter is presented through the lecture.

Along with this *knowledge* aim however, there is also a *comprehension* aim. A good lecturer seeks to interpret and clarify facts which he has presented or which have been learned inductively by the students, perhaps in advance of class.

Still a third goal is *the structuring of material*. The necessity of organization and logic in the lecture is apparent. Students unfamiliar with certain material may discover that the best preliminary exposure available to them is an enthusiastic overview presented by a teacher who has mastered the content and is able to communicate it in a lucid and interesting manner.

Values of the Lecture Method

A good lecture may cover the most material in the least amount of time. Given the proper audio equipment, it lends itself to groups of almost any size and can be handled with a minimum mastery of material on the part of the lecturer.

For example, one does not have to be an Old Testament scholar to present a fairly comprehensive lecture on Psalm 23. Obviously since the total context of that psalm is the entire Bible, one would be a better lecturer if he had competence in all of the Old Testament Scriptures, but such competence is not necessary.

In a lecturing situation the class is likely to stay centered on the subject matter at hand. The teacher is always in charge of the content, and relevant information about the lesson can be clarified and codified.

Lecture is a significant supplement to the printed page. As a college professor clarifies elements in the subject matter which confused the student who read his assignment before coming to class, so the Sunday School teacher explains and applies materials from the lesson manual or the Bible itself.

The good lecturer can also adapt to the needs, interests, abilities, and previous knowledge of his students. He can tie his information into contemporary issues and use realistic illustrations to make the lecture attractive. Such a lecture tends to channel the thinking of all students in a prescribed direction and can be organized either in the logical pattern of subject content or the psychological approach of interest-catching structure.

Problems of the Lecture Method

Unfortunately when misused, as it often is, a lecture can be boring. Any monological approach to the communication of information tends to lead even the best teacher into a rut. An overemphasis on one-way communication also violates some of the basic principles of teaching such as involvement and the motivation of group participation.

Some elements of learning such as attitudes, skills, and feelings are not best learned through "telling" procedures. The lecture can often encourage only the retention of facts as an end itself. What we really need is a translation of biblical information into the life of the student.

Successive use of lecturing tends to encourage acceptance of the teacher as the final authority for truth. This has both theological and pedagogical drawbacks. Theologically it detracts from the supremacy of Scripture as the only rule of faith and practice. The Bible is *the authority;* the teacher is only the agent through whom that authority is communicated.

Pedagogically, transmissive teaching tends to stifle creativity and initiative on the part of the student. There may be very little provision for individual differences, and students' questions often go unanswered. Lecturing often gives a class little opportunity for problem-solving activities and may encourage a passive type of learning.

Communication theorists have told us that feedback is absolutely essential for the completion of the communication cycle. Unless the lecturer is skillfull at reading nonverbal feedback or builds in some kind of verbal feedback as a support methodology for his lecturing, he will have great difficulty discerning student reaction and therefore accurately programming his continuing remarks.

Principles of Effective Lecturing

Here are eight simple ways in which you can improve your teaching if you use the lecture method. Many teachers of adults find themselves making good use of the lecture method. Try some of these suggestions to enhance the value of what can be a valid approach to teaching.

Combine the lecture with audience involvement methods such as discussion, reaction groups, or a question and answer period. This allows for feedback and gives the lecturer opportunity to clarify any concepts which might not have been understood by his audience.

Support the lecture with visuals such as the chalkboard, overhead projector, or charts of various kinds. Often these things are simple and inexpensive to make and yet can increase learning measurably.

Have a *clear and simple outline* for the lecture. Some of the basic rules of homiletics (the art and science of preaching) apply to lecturing as a teaching method. Progressive organization, a clear-cut introduction and conclusion, and parallelism in the outline points will help to make the lecture a better tool for communicating truth.

Practice good principles of speaking such as eye contact, voice inflection, and proper posture.

Emphasize the important points. This may be done as part of the outline itself, but it is often helpful to make an extra effort to insure that students have understood the crucial points of any Bible lesson.

Use interesting illustrations. Illustrations are stories or quotations which "let in the light." They should not be overused, but in proper balance they are a necessary ingredient in the lecture recipe. When a point is otherwise difficult to understand, an illustration should be applied to let students see how that particular concept applies in a real life situation.

Specify clear objectives for the lecture. Actually this is a principle of all good teaching regardless of the methodology. But if you really understand what you want your students to learn as a result of your lecture, you will be able to teach for that goal and come closer to accomplishing the learning objectives. Wasn't it Socrates who said, "We have a much better chance of hitting the target if we can see it"?

Give your students a *mimeographed outline* or guide to follow while you are lecturing. This is not a manuscript. As a matter of fact, the outline should be just detailed enough to enable them to see how you are proceeding in the presentation of the material, but empty enough so that they can take notes during the lecture.

Some students were asked what they liked in lecturers. They listed a sense of humor, a conversational tone, a genuine interest in students, and understandable terminology. Certainly these things can help us be better lecturers.

2
Tell Me
a Story

An influential American educator once said, "Let me tell the stories and I care not who writes the textbooks." Storytelling is one of the oldest forms of transmitted culture. Because of its impact in many societies throughout the ages, it may also have been the most formative element in culture. In his book *The Lonely Crowd,* David Reisman reminds us that "storytellers are indispensable agents of socialization. They picture the world of a child and thus give both form and limits to his memory and imagination" (Yale University Press, New Haven, Conn.).

The history of storytelling reveals that a decline began in the Gutenberg era with the invention of the printing press. However, about 1900 there was a great revival of storytelling as the world realized and began to study its values.

For the Christian of course, Jesus Christ represents the highlight of history with respect to storytelling. The use of stories by our Lord was such a prominent feature that on one occasion Mark records in his Gospel, "And He was not speaking to them without parables" (Mark 4:34, NASB). The Christian teacher who looks to his Lord for a model will neither minimize the value of storytelling as a teaching technique nor relegate it to the world of children. Adults enjoy stories just as children do.

Stories have an inherent value because they can bring pleasure, develop a feeling of fellowship and community, and fix attitudes of appreciation. Stories also act as a governing device for social control. They arouse enthusiasm, project flights of imagination, and accomplish all this while instructing.

Values of Storytelling

Because it carries its own element of interest and attention focusing, storytelling is a very acceptable method of teaching. Stories provide information and enjoyment. When we tell Bible stories, we are teaching truth in such a way that the listener enjoys learning. Stories can help fulfill human needs for love, belonging, and security. A story provides a vicarious experience, allowing the listener to put himself into the situation, thus experiencing its excitement and application.

When viewed in terms of the development of our students, stories offer an opportunity to build personality. They implant proper ideals by showing that certain courses of conduct bring happiness whereas other choices lead to unhappy results. Emotions are stimulated, and that is good because what a person *feels* is always a force in the determination of his behavior. In terms of communicating truth, stories can be used to explain concepts which are not clear in straight exposition.

Problems of Storytelling

Most of the weakness of storytelling centers in its misuse rather than its use. Storytelling tends to look easy, a disguise which deceives the unskilled and unprepared teacher. Such a teacher destroys the effectiveness of the technique in any number of ways:
1. By reading the story instead of telling it
2. By using language which does not clearly communicate meaning
3. By including too many details and "bogging down" a story
4. By overemphasizing minor details and thereby obscuring the basic implication
5. By rote memorization which leads to a mechanical presentation
6. By "sermonizing" the implication rather than letting it find its natural place in the story

7. By offering the story in an atmosphere of stuffiness rather than empathetic enthusiasm
8. By using visual aids as a crutch rather than training facial expressions and body movements to serve as the primary visual support of the story
9. By poor organization which does not allow the story to progress systematically to its logical climax

Principles of Effective Storytelling

A good story is full of action and life. It attracts students by its appeal and then captures them in the instructional resources which it contains. Let us think about the principles of storytelling under these three headings.

Preparation may be the most significant aspect of the storytelling process. The unprepared teacher can do great injustice to *any* valid teaching method. In the first place, preparation certainly includes the selection of the proper story. Good preparation requires the storyteller to know the situation, know the students, and of course know his story. It also requires that he have clear cut objectives for that story so that clearly defined learning patterns can result.

Although occasionally attended by deliberate hyperbole, the story should be accurate and honest without unnecessary embellishments which detract from the central message. Proper organization of the story also must take place in the preparation stage. Most educators agree that there are three basic parts to any story: the introduction, the main body, and the application.

The class also must be prepared for the story experience. The students should be comfortable, with plenty of fresh air and leg room, and as free from distraction as possible. Do not let your departmental superintendent come walking into the class in the middle of the story to collect the offering or the attendance records!

Preparation melts into *presentation* as you begin the first words of the story. In a sense you are still preparing the audience for what is to follow. You are capturing their attention and giving them something to anticipate. You are conscious about important things like eye contact, making an effort to look right into the eyes of all of your students as you tell your story. Let each one believe that you are telling the story just to him.

Make sure everyone can hear every word, but not by shouting all of the time. Sometimes a deliberate quietness will create an enthusiasm for hearing which a high degree of volume could never produce. You might be sitting on the floor, on a chair, or standing to tell the story. Whichever it is, make sure that all of you is telling the story, and not just your mouth.

Subordinate your own personality to that of the main protagonist of the story. Guard against distractions and disturbing mannerisms such as playing with glasses, swaying back and forth, or nervous pacing.

Make sure that your vocabulary is adapted to the understanding level of your class. Use words which describe active sensory experience such as *fuzzy* or *shiny*. Exaggerate your enunciation and speak with enthusiastic animation. Do not be afraid to use dialogue, carefully planned pauses, mimicking of voices, and important sounds.

Of course *prayer* permeates all good Christian teaching. Ask God to help you select the right story, master it thoroughly, and then present it to your class in the power of the Holy Spirit. Expect the God at whose command you teach to involve Himself effectively in your life and the lives of your listeners.

God must like stories. He gave many of them in the Bible. His further approval of the methodology is exemplified in the ministry of His Son on earth. Pray that the precious students who listen to your stories will see in you "a teacher come from God."

Storytelling is a method which increases instructional productivity. Our teaching should get results in the lives of our students. Sometimes those results will be easily measured as in a simple test of certain areas of Bible knowledge, or in the ability to "tell back" the story to the teacher. Such learning is very legitimate. There are, however, behavioral results which are not so easily observed and seem to actually defy testing. How do you really measure whether a primary child has learned to love his friends more as a result of your fine story about the Good Samaritan? How long might a teacher have to wait to see if a story about Cain and Abel will produce new understanding of worship and heart attitude toward God in her children?

Yet we are engaged in teaching for these spiritual goals all the time. We dare not think that just because a story is fun (and many times it ought to be), it should not be measured by the standards which we apply to all methodology. Christian education should make life-change one of the constantly guarded goals of any teaching methodology.

Can storytelling stand up to this kind of a challenge? Of course it can. The parabolic ministry of our Lord is a clear-cut example of storytelling methodology geared to productivity in the lives of His listeners. Remember the kingdom parables of Matthew 13? The Bible tells us that our Lord had a two-fold purpose in these short stories. The disciples were to find in them further help and understanding of Christ's mission in the world and how it affected them. The unbelievers, on the other hand, were to be further confused by His teaching. The unfolding of the rest of the Gospel demonstrates that these objectives were realized. May the Holy Spirit enable us to adopt such a serious posture with respect to the dynamic of this teaching method.

3
Teaching Through
Role Playing

The presently popular technique, role playing, traces back to the psychotherapy of the 1930s. From that narrow beginning, role playing has spread to many and varied forms of education from the primary levels of the elementary school to the upper echelons in managerial training of business executives.

Many teachers confuse role playing and drama. Although they are similar, they are also very distinct in style. Perhaps the most strategic point of difference is the handling of the subject matter: genuine drama usually requires a script, whereas role playing retains the element of spontaneous or at least extemporaneous reaction.

Role may be defined as the way one behaves in a given position and situation. In managerial science, discrepancies in the identificational role are referred to as "role conflict" — inconsistent prescriptions held for a person by himself or by others. Role playing as a teaching methodology is the conscious acting out and discussion of the role in a group. In the classroom a problem situation is briefly acted out so that the individual student can identify with the characters.

A few years ago one of my seminary classes had a unique experience in role playing. It points up the dynamics which can accompany this teaching methodology. Small groups in the class had been assigned to demonstrate various teaching methods in class. The group on role playing set up a situation in which one member played the role of a young man seriously injured in an automobile accident. The only other role was God's attempting to explain to the now rebellious young man how His plan included this catastrophe though the young fellow was about to enter Christian college and give his life for the ministry.

The group arranged the chairs of the class in a circle. In the center, two chairs were set facing each other and unrehearsed dialogue proceeded. The young man shouted at God because of what had happened to him. The calm response of the other player and the progress of the dialogue created a dynamic of learning which those present will not soon forget.

Values of Role Playing

Role playing can be used with students of most ages. The complexity of the role situations must be minimized in using the method with children. But if we keep it simple for their limited attention spans, role playing can be used even in teaching preschoolers.

Role playing allows people to make mistakes in a nonthreatening environment. They can test several solutions to very realistic problems, and the application is immediate. It also fulfills some of the very basic principles of the teaching-learning process such as learner involvement and intrinsic motivation. A positive climate often results in which one can see himself as others see him.

The involvement of the role playing participants can create both an emotional and intellectual attachment to the subject matter at hand. If a skillful teacher has accurately matched the problem situation to the needs of his group, the solving of realistic life problems can be expected.

Role playing can often create a sense of community within the class. Although at first it may seem a threatening method, once the class learns to share a mutual confidence and commitment to the learning process, the sharing of analysis over the role situations will develop a camaraderie never possible in monological teaching methods such as the lecture.

Problems in Role Playing

Perhaps the major drawback to teaching by role playing is the insecurity of class members. Some may react negatively to participating in a situation which will be discussed and possibly criticized by other members of the class. And role playing takes time. The class discussion of a five-to-ten-minute role playing situation may extend to several times the length of the situation itself. Sometimes extremely beneficial results may accrue. At other times, because of ineffective performance on the part of the players, or mishandling on the part of an unprepared teacher, the outcome may only be a superficial rehash of what everyone already knows about the problem.

The relationship of the people in the group is a crucial factor in the success of role playing. At times it may emerge as a negative factor. For example, previous interpersonal difficulties experienced by group members may arise in class to corrupt the role playing situation. Also, if the group has people of different status, they may be reluctant to become involved for fear of being humiliated before the members of the class who are smarter or more popular.

These difficulties with the method are formidable, but they are not insurmountable. Nor are they so extensive that they should prohibit us from experimenting with role playing. The potential benefits of the method quickly overbalance the difficulties which seem so apparent in the initial preparation stages.

Principles for Effective Role Playing

As a teaching technique, role playing is based on the philosophy that *meanings are in people,* not in words or symbols. If that philosophy is accurate, we must first of all *share* the meanings, then *clarify* our understandings of each other's meanings, and finally, if necessary, *change* our meanings.

In the language of phenomenological psychology, this has to do with changing the self concept. The self concept is best changed through direct involvement in a realistic and life-related problem situation rather than through hearing about such situations from others.

Creating a teaching situation which can lead to the change of self concepts requires a *distinct organizational pattern.* One helpful structure for role playing follows:

1. Preparation
   a. Define the problem
   b. Create a readiness for the role(s)
   c. Establish the situation
   d. Cast the characters
   e. Brief and warm up
   f. Consider the training
2. Playing
   g. Acting
   h. Stopping
   i. Involving the audience
   j. Analyzing the discussion
   k. Evaluating

Although we do not have time to explore each of these in detail, it is important to note that all of them focus on group experiences rather than on unilateral behavior of the teacher. The group should share in the defining of the problem, carrying out the role playing situation, discussing the results, and evaluating the whole experience.

The teacher must *identify the situation clearly* so that both the characters and the audience understand the problem at hand. In casting the characters, the wise teacher will try to accept volunteers rather than assign roles. Students must realize that acting ability is not at stake here but rather the spontaneous discharge of how one thinks the character of his role would react in the defined situation.

Players may be instructed publicly so that the audience knows what to expect or privately so that the audience can interpret the meaning of their behavior. Be sure to allow for creativity of the actors within their character roles and do not overstructure the situation.

The discussion and analysis of the role playing situation depends upon how well we involve the audience. Key questions may be asked by the leader and/or buzz groups may be formed. All members of the group (actors and the audience) should participate, and the reactions of the actors may be profitably compared to those of the audience.

The audience is just as much involved in the learning situation as the actors are. In the analysis and discussion time, the audience should provide possible solutions to the realistic problem situations which surface.

It is important to *evaluate role playing* in the light of the prescribed goals. Categorizing behavior is often overdone and gets in the way of the learning process. Evaluation should proceed on both group and personal levels, raising questions concerning the validity of the original purpose.

Throughout the entire process it will be necessary to deal with certain problems which arise in role playing situations. The backward, silent member must be encouraged to contribute. Create an atmosphere in which he is unafraid to share ideas, confident that no one will laugh at his contributions or harshly criticize his conclusions.

The overbearing monopolizer must be curtailed in the discussion phase of role playing lest he dominate the group and thereby quash the dynamic. Solving this problem may require some personal counseling outside of class. Tension and conflict in the group may not always be bad. Sometimes these elements act as a stimulant to thinking. There is such a thing as "creative tension," and it is frequently found in a role playing situation as group dynamic emerges.

At the end of the discussion time the group should collectively measure its effectiveness in reaching biblical solutions to the role problem posed at the beginning. The techniques of role playing afford another approach to involving students in their own learning process toward the clarification of self concepts, evaluation of behavior, and aligning of that behavior with reality. You can see why this is a desirable approach to classroom procedure for the Christian teacher. Prayerfully used under the guidance of the Holy Spirit, role playing can be an effective instrument in the Christian classroom.

4
Techniques
of the Scripture Search

One of the primary purposes of Christian teaching at any level and any place is to enable students to become independent investigators of the Word of God. Too much Bible knowledge in evangelical churches today is secondhand. It stems from listening to pastors and teachers but rarely if ever from analyzing the Word of God inductively.

One of the ways to teach inductive Bible study is by means of a method called "Scripture search." This methodology enables students to learn *how* to use their Bibles by *using* them in class under the guidance of a teacher who is himself an independent investigator of God's truth.

Scripture search may employ several approaches such as the *springboard* (analyzing subject matter from a textual point of view); *deductive* (developing a systematic theology on the basis of various passages); or *inductive* (analyzing the particulars of a given passage of Scripture leading to the forming of a conclusion). Few Bible scholars would question that the inductive approach is the best technique in leading students to learn how to use the Bible for themselves.

Inductive Bible study assumes that any person who can read and is reasonably intelligent will be able to grasp the content and meaning of Scripture. The meaning will in turn lead him to the knowledge of how God expects him to think and live. Scripture itself asserts that on the basis of one's own Bible study he may discern God's truth. The Christians at Berea illustrated this principle and were commended by the Apostle Paul for examining "the Scriptures daily, whether those things were so" (Acts 17:11).

Inductive study differs from the deductive method by not prejudging the meaning and application of any particular passage. Correct theology becomes the result, not the presupposition, of the inquiry. Instead of dividing the Bible into verses, the study proceeds book by book as the Bible was written.

It is important to note that in using the Scripture search, both medium and message are important. We want to communicate the subject matter in a given lesson. However, we also want to demonstrate *how* the same approach to Bible study can be applied to other subject matter in another time and place. In studying a lesson on John 15, the student should learn not only the scriptural teaching about the vine and the branches, but also how to apply the approaches used in that class to a study of John 16, Acts 21, or any other passage of Scripture.

Values of Scripture Search

In addition to seeing the biblical text and hearing it read, students should enter into a firsthand investigation of the *meaning* as well as the words of the Bible. Since a good Scripture search also incorporates the methodology of discussion, people tend to share meanings. They measure each other's understanding not by what the teacher says but by what they are finding in the Word of God itself. Educators generally agree that students learn better when they discover truth for themselves rather than having it prechewed by someone else.

The writer of the Book of Hebrews reacted negatively to the maturity level of his readers. At a time when they should have been instructors of others, they were still needing explanation of the most elementary truths of God. In Sunday Schools all across the world, we are perpetuating this problem rather than solving it. Students are not learning how to study the Bible because their teachers often do not know how to study the Bible.

Through the application of the careful use of Scripture search methodology, teacher and student will learn together how to come directly to the fountain of God's truth for necessary living water. This can happen not only in the classroom group setting, but also in private and individual patterns of Bible study.

For some years my wife has taught a ladies Bible study class on Thursday afternoons. Frequently the class is attended by women who are unsaved but who display a genuine interest in knowing what the Word of God has to say. On one occasion as they were working through Mark, one of the unsaved women interrupted by pointing to a certain verse in the passage and exclaiming, "If this verse means what I think it means, I'm not a Christian." The piercing truth of the Word had done its work. None of the other ladies had attempted overt evangelism but had allowed the Word of God to speak for itself. This is precisely the approach we should be taking in Scripture search.

Problems in Scripture Search

There may be fewer inherent weaknesses in Scripture search than in methodology which depends more upon the activity of teachers or students. This teaching method tends to be more Bible-centered and less man-centered. Nevertheless there are some dangerous pitfalls to be avoided when using the Scripture search.

One of the most common problems is closed-mindedness. We have a tendency to come to a given passage of Scripture with the assumption that we already know what it says. Our study becomes nothing more than a superficial review of preconceived ideas. Because genuine inductive Bible study tends to destroy mistaken notions, it can appear dangerous to the outward harmony of the group. Having taken offense at a particular biblical viewpoint agreed on by the majority of the class, some people may be sufficiently disturbed that they will not return to your class or church.

Another hang-up facing us in this approach to teaching is the temptation to minimize the necessity of preparation. If the leader's structured questions are not thoughtful, the group might be hindered in getting the spiritual meaning and relevant application of the passage. By the same token, the questions themselves may be prejudicial, precluding any genuine understanding of what the passage really says.

All of the problems of the discussion method apply to Scripture search with an even greater impact. For example, a dominant group member currently riding a theological hobbyhorse may distort the group's understanding of a scriptural point. The skillful teacher must ward off any efforts to do so. Furthermore, the sharing of life experiences by the group's more vocal members may become a threat rather than an encouragement to the timid members of the group. Honest group induction can degenerate into an occasion for exhibiting spiritual trophies. Also, the encouragement of freedom and spontaneity should not lead to excessive levity or lack of reverence for God's holy Word.

Principles for Effective Scripture Search

Essential to all inductive Bible study is an understanding of the three crucial questions which must be answered about any passage of Scripture we approach:

1. What does it say?
2. What does it mean?
3. What does it have to do with me?

Answering these questions for each passage (chapter paragraph, verse, or word) can be facilitated by observing the following guidelines:

As the teacher you must be sufficiently *familiar with the material* to steer the discussion. Your response to the passage will affect the dynamics of the discussion and may lead (or mislead) group members to conclusions.

Make sure that the answers to the questions always *center in Scripture*. Inductive Bible study is not a sharing of opinions by members of the group. It is not a pooling of theological ignorance. Every suggestion of meaning must be subjected to the searchlight of God's Word as the Holy Spirit leads us into truth.

Try to *keep the group small* enough to be flexible for discussion and interaction. Arrange the chairs in a circle so that the concept of sharing is reflected even in the physical arrangement of the room.

Stay away from reference works including marginal notes. The suggestions of the commentators may come later, but now use your own initiative and thoughts under the guidance of the Holy Spirit. Remember that Christ promised, "He will guide you into all truth" (John 16:13).

Make sure that the three questions of inductive Bible study are approached in the *right order*. Groups will sometimes want to dash right on to the application stage before the factual data of the text has been established. In order to avoid this problem, the teacher must frequently (at least in the early usages of this method) clarify the observation-interpretation-application procedure.

Avoid becoming too goal oriented. All good teaching proceeds on the basis of clear and specific objectives, but in this kind of methodology there must be sufficient room for flexibility so that the group itself does the work. *They* find the facts. *They* determine the meaning. And *they* discuss how this portion of God's Word has significance for them in their pressure-cooker world.

Certainly there is direction from the teacher, particularly with respect to keeping the group in the text. But Scripture search methodology exhibits a genuine dependence on the working of the Holy Spirit in the group and an expectation that honest commitment to His leading and to the text itself will lead to truth.

When approaching a passage which is not in some sequence of study, *sketch the context first* so that the group may determine the situation in which these words were spoken or written. It is essential that the sketch not contain interpretive overtones or the basic inductive technique will be corrupted. For example, think of a lesson on John 11 which you intend to teach using Scripture search methodology. If the class has not been studying the Gospel of John, you may need to introduce the procedure by saying, "In our passage Jesus is confronted with the death of a close friend. This incident happened late in His ministry, when the animosity of the Jews was already at a high pitch." You would *not* say, "This chapter teaches us that every Christian will experience bodily resurrection because of the power and promise of Christ." The passage may well teach that, but this methodology puts the privilege of that discovery upon the class.

Teachers willing to use Scripture search will soon discover a vibrancy and vitality unmatched by most other methods.

5
Teaching
by Discussion

Discussion teaching differs from question and answer teaching primarily by the kind of questions used. In discussion it is our purpose to get students to think through the issues rather than verbalize memorized data or repeat right answers. Most often discussion will center on the solution to a problem or perhaps the interpretation of a verse of Scripture. Discussion can also be thought of as an attempt to interact with others toward arriving at a solution based on thoughts and ideas expressed by members of the group.

In the Christian classroom, thoughts and ideas are not merely opinions based on personal experience or perhaps prejudice. Rather, they are understandings of the meaning of those portions of Scripture which have a bearing on the problem at hand. All those meanings are made clearer to the discussants by the ministry of the Holy Spirit ("He will guide you into all truth," John 16:13).

Basic to a good discussion is a problem which is clearly defined. The problem must be limited in scope so that it can be understood by members of the group and satisfactorily dealt with in the allotted time. When used as a teaching method, discussion is not conducted for the sake of therapy but rather for the sake of pinpointing answers and solutions.

As the group approaches the problem(s) at hand, the members seek to analyze the issues involved in the light of biblical evidence. Possible solutions may be presented by the members of the group as they weigh and consider ideas and viewpoints. Through this process a line of reasoning or logical thought should emerge and lead to one or more solutions to the problem.

These solutions are then examined to determine their validity and implications. Remember that discussion is not debate. It is not the purpose of the class to "win" an argument or to establish one way of thinking. Teacher and students are engaged in a cooperative effort to seek for truth, knowing in advance that truth and its application to life can be found in God's Word.

Values of the Discussion Method
Teaching by discussion utilizes one of the best principles of the learning process, namely, the involvement of students in active participation in the learning experience. A good discussion will help students express themselves verbally, crystalize their thinking in conjunction with the thinking of their peers, and develop a tolerance for those with whom they may disagree.

Management research teaches us that people change most rapidly and completely in proportion to the amount of interaction which they have with other people. People who tend to isolate themselves physically or mentally will become set in their ways and resist innovation in their lives or thought patterns. On the other hand, people who engage in open exchange of ideas with others will learn both the existence and validity of other points of view and will more readily moderate, or perhaps even drastically change, their own ideas.

Teaching by discussion is a motivational technique which encourages a student to think through concepts which have been hazy. Wrong conclusions may be corrected through the influence of the group rather than the unilateral actions of the teacher. Problem-solving techniques are learned which can be applied not only in the search for knowledge, but in all aspects of life. Creative thinking may also be stimulated.

A discussion setting also provides an atmosphere which can enhance group rapport and camaraderie. The informality of the situation (when properly conducted) allows group members to sense how other people feel, and identification with the group begins to emerge. In a good discussion session, one soon learns that the questions which have been bothering him are not unique but are problems faced by many of his friends. The humanness and concern of the teacher comes through much more clearly in a discussion than it can in a lecture.

One of the essential factors in the communication process is the securing of feedback. In lecturing or storytelling the teacher is dependent upon nonverbal feedback (unless he can combine those methods with supportive dialogical techniques). In discussion, however, if the teacher is asking the right questions and soliciting genuine thought and honest expression on the part of the class, he will soon learn whether they understand the subject matter or further clarification is necessary. Good discussion questions will capture a mind that might wander to more attractive mental pastures during a monological form of teaching.

Problems of the Discussion Method

Small group study is very popular in the church today. Yet it detracts from our purposes when it becomes a *substitute for* rather than a *supplement to* the proclamation of the Word of God. Some want to avoid such a dangerous tendency by steering away from dialogical teaching altogether. But such a reactionary swing of the pendulum is also unfortunate. Discussion teaching does not have to degenerate to a pooling of ignorance. Only two things are necessary to avoid this problem: a teacher-guide who genuinely knows how to use the Bible; and a commitment on the part of the group members to search for biblical answers rather than experiential opinions to problems.

Another possible drawback to teaching by discussion is the amount of time required to cover any given amount of material. It will take longer to teach the same material by the discussion method than by the lecture method. On the other hand, students will be learning *technique* as well as *content,* and both the retention and comprehension levels may be markedly increased because of participation in the interaction. But discussion does take time, and the teacher who is intent on "getting over the lesson" will not be as committed to teaching by discussion as the teacher who wants to "get the lesson over."

Sometimes reticent or bashful students may be embarrassed in a discussion situation. This may be true of an entire class on occasion if that class has not had opportunity to experience dialogical teaching techniques. Teachers should be careful not to publicly humiliate a student by asking an unusually difficult question or forcing his involvement when he clearly does not wish to participate.

Rambling or wandering from the subject at hand is another common problem in many discussion situations. Here again the leadership of the teacher is essential. Sometimes teachable moments will arise, and the teacher will deliberately allow discussion to wander into a bypath that might seem profitable for learning. Generally, however, he will keep the group from being diverted.

Some teachers feel safer with the lecture method. If a teacher has only a shallow understanding of the subject or has prepared inadequately, he will be threatened by the possibility that students may ask questions he cannot answer. Many teachers are insecure in their classroom situations and find safety in a kind of teaching which allows them to stick strictly to "the script" and avoid having to think on their feet. Most teachers fear discussion, however, because they simply do not know how to employ the techniques.

A class should be reasonably small in order to use the discussion method. To involve the entire class with as many as possible participating in a given hour, 20 to 25 students is probably the maximum number for effectiveness. However, there are various subcategories of discussion teaching which can be used with much larger numbers. These will be discussed as separate teaching methods in this book.

Principles for Effective Discussion Teaching
Probably one of the most important factors in securing a good discussion is *framing the problem or question*. Just getting people to talk does not guarantee that a genuine learning-by-discussion situation is in effect. Application of biblical truth is essential. The questions themselves must be worded to produce

thought rather than factual response. Many good discussion-type questions begin with the words *why* or *how*.

The *arrangement of the room* is a significant factor in discussion. Although it is possible to have effective discussion with participants in rows or pews, the group dynamics necessary are more likely to be achieved by the use of a circle. The teacher should be part of the circle, sitting with the students to engage in "the cooperative search for truth."

Attitudes are very important in discussion teaching. The teacher must have the disposition of a co-learner rather than that of a lecturer or a scholar. He must be a goad and guide rather than a teller and transmitter. The attitude of all group members must be one of receptivity and openness to new ideas. They should not be afraid to share ideas, confident that no one will laugh at their contributions or harshly criticize their conclusions.

About 10 years ago I was conducting a Christian Education Conference in a church in downstate Illinois. At the last minute I was asked to teach a young adult Sunday School class. I decided to attempt a dialogical approach, just to see what would happen. My first question, "What have you been studying this quarter?" brought no response whatever from the 20 young adults. I then asked, "Is it in the Old Testament or the New Testament?" I still got no response. After two or three more questions a lady in the back row timidly raised her hand and volunteered a piece of information.

That class was communicating to me their ideas of what Sunday School ought to be. It was clearly a place where the students sat and listened while the teacher spoke. Classes like this do not change their attitudes easily nor quickly.

It will be essential to *deal with certain problems* which arise in discussion situations. The silent member must be encouraged to contribute. The overbearing monopolizer must be curtailed in his efforts to dominate the group. Solving this problem may require some personal counseling outside of the classtime itself. Tension and conflict in the group may not always be bad. Sometimes these elements help stimulate thinking.

Do not forget *evaluation*. At the end of the discussion time, the group should collectively measure its effectiveness in reaching biblical solutions to the problems posed at the beginning.

The technique itself should be evaluated, seeking ways in which procedures could be improved the next time. Sometimes it is helpful for group members to talk about how they felt when certain ideas were introduced or certain conclusions drawn by the group.

The modern church which employs the small discussion group in its instructional organization will go far toward establishing the type of personally focused group life which gave the Gospel its start in the world. Christian education has been effective where the small group was vitalized by a Christian personality able to communicate biblical truth to others with warmth of spirit and depth of insight. Can you be that kind of teacher?

6
Questions
and Answers

Involving a class in questions and answers is the first step away from monological teaching. It is the initial recognition that learning takes place when students are verbally as well as intellectually involved in the educational situation. Here we are attempting to secure verbal interaction. Actually interaction may be of several types and is essential to all learning. Most educators agree that mental interaction is not sufficient but should be accompanied by some form of student expression or reaction. The student must comprehend truth in his own mind, then express it in his own words.

Question and answer teaching gives the student the opportunity to reflect his inquiries and needs for further information. At the same time, by soliciting answers to key questions the teacher gains some insight into the class' progress.

Can we really take time to allow the student to insert his questions? After all, the teaching session is short, and we have much objective truth to communicate! The basis for questions and answers in Christian teaching can be traced to the ministry of our Lord, who frequently utilized this technique both as a complete methodology in itself, and as a supplement to other types of methodology. Although Marshall McLuhan may argue that the "medium is the message," the Christian educator may counter that the message controls the medium. To put it another way, what we have to say will have a profound influence on how we say it. Dr. Clifford Anderson of Bethel Seminary writes that "methods may be likened to bridges or roadways that are employed by persons who are concerned to assist others to an objective. They are means to an end. Our experiences in Christ and His body, the Church, give rise to mission which in turn stimulates interest in method." Methods must therefore be both theologically accurate and educationally adequate. The question and answer method can meet both these requirements.

Values of the Question and Answer Approach

Although the use of questions does not automatically produce effective teaching, adequate use of the question and answer method will greatly facilitate communication. Along with satisfying the need for involvement, this approach to teaching also solicits feedback. By asking questions we can determine whether people are understanding what we are teaching and whether the message of Scripture is being properly applied to contemporary life.

The human mind naturally tends to explore the unknown and to express curiosity about things which seem different or strange. Consider the many times a child may say, "Why, Daddy?" Think of the varied and significant questions asked our Lord by His disciples. Questions and answers direct a pupil's attention toward the lesson content. When a response is required, we have aroused not only the attention of the individual student, but also the attention of the entire class. Questions can be used for drill and review; they deepen impressions and fix facts in the mind and memory of the student.

Inviting students to participate by asking questions also prompts them to think that it is *their* class rather than *your* class. Such identification with the teaching-learning experience may well produce additional motivation and increase the student's learning level.

Problems in Using Questions and Answers

The use of questions and answers in class is a perfectly legitimate approach to teaching, but it is often confused with discussion. As indicated in the last chapter, perhaps the best way to make a distinction is to emphasize *the kind of question involved.* Question and answer teaching almost always deals with factual data and objective responses. Very often it is a review of material previously studied by the students, or just covered in a lecture or story. Although thought questions can certainly be used in this approach to teaching, there is a tendency in a thought question to pose a defined problem and thereby lapse over to the discussion technique. Both of these techniques are perfectly valid, but the teacher should be able to identify when he is using discussion and when he is using question and answer.

A common weakness in question and answer teaching is the framing of superfluous or shallow questions which offer no challenge to the class. The use of a rhetorical question, for example, is a worthy device for communication but is not a proper approach to question and answer teaching. Sufficient "mystery" about the answer helps motivate a genuinely intellectual response on the part of the student.

Furthermore, the use of questions should not ·be viewed as a substitute for knowledge of the material or communication of important content. Questions cannot impart objective data and are not well used to accomplish such teaching goals.

Sometimes teachers spend too much of the classtime asking questions and too little listening to questions. But how can you get your class to talk? The problem of silence generally lies in one of three areas: their past educational pattern has conditioned them to sit and listen but not to participate verbally in the classtime; their lack of interest in the subject creates a "ho-hum" atmosphere so that no questions are motivated; their ignorance of answers to your questions forces them to hide behind a shield of silence lest their lack of study or inability to produce be unmasked.

Principles for Improving Questions and Answers
Like all good teaching, the question and answer technique is *planned in advance,* it does not just happen in the classtime. The teacher decides what kind of issues can be framed in questions and uses the approach in review, in introduction of new

material, or in testing whether the class has understood the material just presented.

Be on the lookout for the teachable moment. Sometimes questions which appear to be off the subject may provoke interest and motivation on the part of the class. A teacher is always a decision maker, and in this situation he must decide whether the answer to the question is of sufficient benefit to the class to take time to deal with it, even though it might not be directly related to the lesson of the hour.

Sometimes it is beneficial to *give students the questions ahead of time* rather than asking them directly in class. This approach is often necessary when weaning a class from a "sitting and sulking" behavior to a participation behavior. The teacher of an adult Sunday School class for example may distribute 3″ by 5″ cards with key questions for next week's lesson. Included on the cards would be some scriptural guidelines for students to do independent research on the questions and be ready to plug in that information during the next class session. Variations like this enhance the use of the question and answer technique.

Teachers should *only ask questions understandable to the student.* The purpose of this technique is not to demonstrate the scholarship of the teacher, nor to display how his superior intelligence can "show up" the comparative ignorance of his students. If a question is not clear to a student, it should be repeated in different verbal forms so that the student can grasp the significance of what is being asked.

The *teacher's respons*e to student questions is also important. Unless it is apparent that the student is deliberately trying to disrupt the class (a situation which is rarely the case), the teacher should recognize each question as one of serious consequence to the student who raised it and treat it with respect. Under no circumstances should a student be made to feel inferior or stupid because of a question or an answer which he offers in class.

Questions can also be used for the sake of *application.* In teaching 1 Corinthians 8, for example, a teacher might ask his students, "What kinds of behavior today do you think would be like their eating meat offered to idols?" or "How does the lesson of this chapter apply to our lives today?"

Although a small matter, it is important for the teacher to *direct the question* to the whole class before specifying the student to answer it. Challenge will soon be extinguished when students know that questions are coming in a certain definable pattern, or if the name of a student is always attached right at the outset.

Never be negative toward a student's response. Even when the wrong answer is given, the good teacher will find some element of truth or commendation to *reinforce the response.*

The effective use of question and answer methodology is inseparably related to a thorough knowledge of the subject matter and careful lesson planning. The teacher who genuinely wants to involve his students in this way will write out questions in advance and test their significance and relevance rather than just flippantly asking whatever comes into his mind during the lesson period.

7
Using Buzz Groups in Your Teaching

Apparently the method known as "buzz groups" was first used by Dr. Donald Phillips at Michigan State University. He would divide his large classes into six-member clusters asking them to discuss a certain problem for six minutes. As you might guess, it was not long until the new approach became known on campus as the "Phillips 66" technique. Now the use of buzz groups is quite popular, and varying formats and arrangements have been introduced to add a great deal of flexibility to this type of discussion teaching.

Because of the flexibility, buzz groups cannot be narrowly defined. The name certainly can be applied whenever a large assembly of people is divided into small groups (usually of no less than three and no more than eight) which for a limited time simultaneously discuss separate problems or various phases of a given problem. If possible, recorders from each of the groups report their findings to the reassembled large group. This technique can be effectively used as early as the Junior Department and increases in significance up to young and middle adulthood.

Frequently buzz groups will follow a lecture, panel, or some other teaching form which has been used to transmit certain basic information about a given subject. The groups can be assigned questions raised by the speaker, or unresolved issues which emerge from the first part of the teaching period.

I'll never forget a situation in which I used buzz groups with a young adult class. As I explained what we would be doing that morning their eyes filled with terror. This new approach seemed threatening to them, and they would much rather have had me take care of all of the performance. The plan was to have them study certain verses of Scripture for about 20 minutes in their buzz groups and then report to the wider group.

Things started slowly, but at the end of the 20 minutes when I informed them that they should "wrap up their findings" and prepare for reports, I had a mini-rebellion on my hands. "Quit? Wind up? Ready to report? Why, we just got started." The thrill of learning had set in. They were hooked. Some of those folks had entered into group Bible studies seriously for the first time in their adult lives.

Herbert A. Thelen, in his book *Dynamics of Groups at Work* (University of Chicago Press, Chicago, Ill.), suggests, "the buzz group offers a natural and useful transition from the listening situation to the decision of each individual to act. It is an intermediate step in the movement of responsibility from the officials (leaders) to the small groups to the individual." He also suggests four other valuable uses for this approach in teaching and group work:

1. To get a meeting started on significant problems with the members assuming considerable responsibility
2. To set up an agenda for a meaningful learning experience
3. To overcome a feeling of helplessness or apathy and to redirect the group toward action
4. To test a set of ideas, and to increase communication between speaker and audience

Flexibility and variation are important factors in the use of buzz groups. Let us look at a Sunday School teacher who exemplifies these qualities.

Jim T. is the teacher of a young adult class. After coming back from a Sunday School convention last month, he decided to put into practice the things he learned in a workshop on buzz groups. His class numbers about 30 and meets in a little prayer chapel. His lesson for Sunday focuses on the personal witnessing techniques of Christ as seen in John 4:1-38. Jim plans to approach his teaching hour this way:

9:45—9:50 Welcome, announcements, and opening prayer.

9:50—10:10 Give a brief explanation of the setting of John 4. This will include showing something of the geographical setting of Samaria in relation to Judea and Galilee. To do this Jim intends to use an overhead projector with prepared maps. He will also briefly touch on the nature of the Samaritans: who they were, where they came from, and what they believed.

10:10—10:15 Explain the following six questions for discussion:

1. What specifically did Christ mean by his reference to "living water?"
2. Why did Jesus bring up the subject of this woman's husbands?
3. What kind of diversion does the woman raise in verse 20, and how does our Lord handle it?
4. What is the meaning of verse 24, and what implications does it have for our worship today?
5. What did Christ mean by His statement, "Lift up your eyes, and look on the fields; for they are white already to harvest" (v. 35)?
6. According to verse 38, how were the disciples involved in this ministry?

10:15—10:30 Chairs will be rearranged into six circles of approximately five people each. A group leader will be appointed whose task it is to keep the discussion on target and involve all the members of the group. He is not to teach or to dominate discussion. Each group will immediately select its own recorder or secretary, who will be responsible for the report.

10:30—10:45 The groups will reassemble, and each reporter will have approximately two minutes to share the findings of his group in answer to the question assigned. Jim may make one or two closing remarks at the end of the hour and then dismiss the class with prayer.

Several things are assumed in Jim's lesson plans. First of all, the Adult Department in his Sunday School has wisely given up its old system of "opening exercises." Each class goes immediately to its classroom, and any preliminaries are taken care of there. Jim does not have to worry about passing around any kind of attendance lists since the class secretary sits in the back of the room and checks the attendance during the first few minutes.

Jim also has the advantage of a room with some privacy and folding chairs which can be moved anywhere he wants to put them. In addition, he has a small enough class so that division into smaller groups is quite workable.

But remember the flexibility angle. Suppose Jim had 60 students instead of 30. If the chairs were still movable and the room large enough, he could have retained his lesson plan with one exception: he would have assigned two groups to each question rather than one.

But let us assume for the moment that Jim had to meet his class in the sanctuary, where they sit in pews rather than folding chairs. Could he have used buzz groups?

Yes, assuming he has had the foresight to bring all of the class members together in one corner of the auditorium rather than letting them spread out. He will still use his same lesson format and the same questions. But now he will go to a variation of buzz groups called either "neighbor nudging," "triads," or "diads." This is a technique which involves two or three people sitting together and discussing a question among themselves. There is no appointed leader, and the teacher may select any one of the two or three to give the informal report.

If his class numbers 60 and Jim wants to keep his original six questions, he might decide to use triads, thus giving him 20 small discussion groups. He would have at least three groups on each question and four groups on two of the questions. The major deficiency here is that he will surely not have time for all of the reports so he will have to select a representative sample. The advantage is that he can use diads or triads with almost any type of room furniture and arrangement in a class of almost any size. Perhaps the diagram on page 47 will more clearly establish the buzz group arrangements discussed above.

Values of Buzz Group Teaching

Buzz group teaching, like other forms of discussion, takes advantage of that significant teaching principle, *interaction*. The class confronts the subject matter firsthand rather than passively receiving what a teacher has to say. Jim could have answered any of

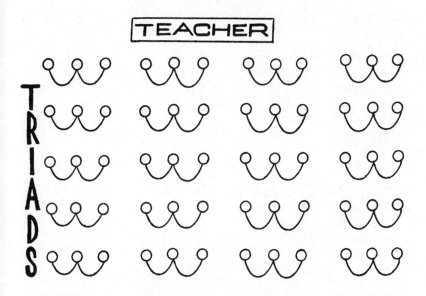

his questions in a lecture, but the answers will be much more meaningful if the class members can find them in the text. Some of the class members would never participate in a discussion if the whole class were listening to their contribution. In the small group, however, the threat is minimized, and people find it easier to express themselves and share their understanding of scriptural issues.

Adaptability is a plus factor for this teaching method. We saw how Jim could adapt if the Sunday School superintendent suddenly moved him into the auditorium. The subject matter is also a flexible item. Buzz groups can deal with interpretation of Scripture, discussion of topical matters, controversial questions raised by a guest speaker, implementation of ideas by the members of the group, and many other types of learning. Sometimes patience and tolerance develop as group members are forced into a situation of listening to what someone else has to say on the subject.

Do not forget the factor of leadership development. Although the roles of group leader and recorder-reporter may not seem very significant at the time, this exposure to the sharing of responsibility for the effectiveness of the class is an important ingredient in the process of training classmembers to be leaders themselves.

Problems in Using Buzz Groups

Sometimes the use of buzz groups will threaten a class. As a matter of fact, the first time you use the technique you should expect your class members to be somewhat afraid of the group interaction. But soon they will discover that learning is enjoyable when the learner is directly involved.

Sometimes the groups will not arrive at the conclusions which the leader might have desired. If he has left himself some time to "pull together" the issues, he may be able to solve this problem. But an honest discussion should not predetermine what conclusions the group is to reach. The process should be as inductive as possible.

Sometimes a weakness shows up in the selection of the group leader. If the leader fails to take the responsibility to keep his group on the subject and to catalytically draw out each member, then the effectiveness of the technique will be in danger.

Buzz groups also take time. Just as in any other kind of discussion teaching, the teacher must plan to invest more time to cover the same amount of material than if he were teaching monologically. But again, the emphasis should be on creating learning in the minds and lives of the students, not necessarily in covering the greatest amount of material in the shortest time.

Principles for Effective Buzz Groups

Some pitfalls can be avoided if the teacher will carefully observe some basic principles which facilitate the effectiveness of buzz group teaching.

Plan the classtime to allow for moving chairs, explaining the technique, and hearing reports. These items will usually take longer than you anticipate.

Make clear to the class what the *roles of group leader and recorder* should be. This is done before the entire group so that everyone will know how he is to react to the leader and recorder in his group.

Set a definite *time limit* for discussion. The general tendency is to think that groups will be able to do more in a certain amount of time than they can actually handle effectively. If five group members have 15 minutes to deal with their question, each member of the group can speak to the question only three minutes.

The *teacher should "float"* from group to group to motivate better involvement, help them over any hurdles, and generally spread enthusiasm around the room.

Gather the notes from the reporters, and prepare a mimeographed sheet of the total findings of the class. The recorders will probably be speaking so fast that no one can take notes. Furthermore, this sheet will give the class a symbol of their own effectiveness in discussion and Bible study. The leader can also add his own comments at the end so that such a report sheet will be helpful as a reference item long after the class is over.

8
The Panel
Discussion

The panel is another approach to discussion teaching. Differing from general discussion, question and answer, and buzz groups, the panel is almost always used with a large group, and generally utilizes panel members who have either differing points of view on the subject or special training and experience which equip them to speak authoritatively about the matter. Properly planned, the panel is a small discussion group performing its discussion before an audience with the objective of giving that audience a better understanding of the matter at issue.

Usually there are no prepared speeches and, in the best panels, interaction between the panel members will make up at least half of the time allotted to the panel's presentation. During that interaction there may be agreement, disagreement, qualification of points, and defense of various positions.

Although the immediate goal is to gain information from a group of experts, if time allows the audience should be encouraged to interact with the panel members. In this way the panel itself becomes more than just a purveyor of information and acts also as a catalyst to get the group to thinking about the issues.

In a one-hour class period you would probably have to allot 10 minutes for introduction of the subject and panel members and

30 minutes for the presentation and discussion by the panel. The remaining 20 minutes can be given to audience reaction. Most of the time a panel discussion is a carefully programmed event built around the expertise of the panel members. Sometimes, however, it is effective to use an "impromptu panel." In this situation panelists chosen from the class speak "off the cuff" on the subject presented to them.

This type of panel can draw out certain opinions and ideas on the subject under consideration rather than offering authoritative information. In any kind of panel the room should be properly arranged so that the panel participants can look at one another while they interact and yet can easily be seen and heard by all members of the audience. Three or four panelists is probably an ideal number. Any more than five would tend to make interaction an elusive goal.

Several variations to the planned panel lend flexibility to its use. Here are three different approaches:
1. The Guided Panel. The moderator addresses previously prepared questions to the panel. Obviously this is a very structured approach, but it may be desirable when the panel members do not know each other or if their points of view are so diverse as to cause open hostility if free interaction were allowed.
2. The Expanding Panel. In this arrangement a preliminary and explanatory discussion of a topic is given by a restricted panel. Then the entire group forms a circle to continue the discussion. In this open discussion time, questions may be addressed to the panel, but discussion might take place also among the group members with panel members serving primarily as resources.
3. The Reaction Panel. In this setting the first thing on the program is a speech, a film, or some other presentation of a point of view. Preselected panel members then offer a critique of the presentation either by speaking briefly to the issue, interacting with the speaker, or both. Sometimes it is helpful if the panel members have the manuscript of the speech in advance or have had opportunity to preview the film. This way their carefully prepared reactions will give birth to some audience thinking which might not have occurred without airing

of the issues by the panel. Reaction panels of newsmen often discuss presidential speeches, for example.

A reaction panel can become an expanding panel if time allows. These classifications are not necessarily mutually exclusive, but rather represent an attempt to clarify different approaches to the use of the panel for education.

Values of Panel Discussions

A good panel discussion can focus attention of the class on what certain experts have to say about the subject at hand. It is considerably more personal then reading books about the subject and contains that important educational ingredient — *interest*. If the topic is well selected, it is relevant, problematic, controversial, and therefore attracts attention immediately. Wise selection of the panel members will offer the audience more than one viewpoint and thereby heighten interest.

Because of the multiplicity of input, the panel discussion offers a breadth and depth of information which usually exceeds research presented by one speaker. The class can realize that well-informed people may hold different points of view and yet maintain respect for one another. The freedom and informality of the panel discussion removes the pressure of having to prepare a structured speech. Panel members literally think aloud in front of the class and collectively move toward a solving of the problem placed before them.

The input of the panel at the beginning of the period gives the audience some foundational information upon which their discussion can proceed. Without the panel, or at least some kind of formal presentation of material, the discussion might degenerate into a pooling of ignorance. With the presence of the panel, however, the discussion period becomes a forum for new ideas and experiences in the lives of the group.

Problems in the Panel Method

Perhaps the biggest weakness in the use of panel discussions is securing competent panelists who will do the job well. Even if a man is an expert in his field, when placed on a panel he may have the tendency to monopolize the time, ramble from the subject, or ride his hobbyhorse. He might ignore the audience and speak in technical jargon to the other panel members or even "lose his cool" in the interaction time, displaying antagonism toward those who disagree with him. Unless he knows his panel members well, the teacher takes some risks in setting up a panel discussion.

Another problem is that panel members may not always do justice to a particular point of view. What happens then is that the class tends to think that position A is better than position B simply because A was defended more competently. They will invariably gravitate toward the effective presentation rather than the position that makes the most sense logically or biblically.

Closely connected with this problem is the possibility of disorganization in the panel. Since ideas and viewpoints are flowing informally, the information often lacks logical sequence and arguments are hard to follow. Sometimes students find it more difficult to listen to a panel than to an individual speaker because of this collage of ideas thrown at them in a short period of time.

Principles for the Effective Use of Panels

Obviously the values of panel discussion as a teaching technique are going to be dependent upon several critical factors. If those factors are not handled positively, the difficulties of the panel may outweigh the benefits. This of course does not have to be the case. The following items are crucial in making the system work. If they can be controlled and positively utilized, the panel discussion will be a very useful teaching method.

The *moderator must be a highly qualified* and competent individual. Without doubt the moderator is more strategic in the effective use of the panel discussion than the panel members themselves. He sets the stage with the initial remarks and keeps the discussion on target during the interaction time. He has the difficult responsibility of calling time on the panel members if a brief period of presentation is afforded each of them.

During the open discussion time, he clarifies questions given by the audience and may also find it necessary to explain answers offered in return by the panel members. If necessary, he may have to break up verbal conflicts before they actually get underway. He prods panel members for reactions to something which another has said, structures questions to keep the flow of information moving, and summarizes the conclusions at the end. All of this is a very difficult task and can mean the success or failure of the panel experience.

The *subject for discussion* should be of importance to the group and worded in the form of a specific question. It is futile, for example, to get a group of experts together for 30 minutes to discuss sex education. One might talk about sex education in the school, another in the home, still another may pull out some biblical aspects of sex. The end result would be a hodgepodge of nothingness because no specific direction was indicated for the panel. The question should rather construct something like this: "Should formal sex education be taught here at First Church?" Even then it will be necessary to define words such as *formal* and *sex education*. The more specific the question, the closer the panel will get toward the goal of problem-solving on the issue.

Try to *load the panel* with different points of view. It will be of no value to the group if every panel member says the same thing, and the time is spent watching them pat each other on their ideological backs. One of the major purposes of a panel is to air different positions. For this reason, it is necessary to bring together persons of similar competence so that those positions will have fair and equal hearings.

Always *allow time for a summary* of the discussion. The summary might take place at two points: immediately after the panel finishes, to pull together ideas which they have presented; and at the end of the expanded session, to crystalize any conclusions which have emerged from the total experience.

Remember that the panel has a much wider use than in the Sunday School class itself. A Sunday evening service, for example, could be very profitably scheduled around a panel of three or four guests who discuss such issues as "Is there a biblical position on abortion?" "What is the distinctive role of the church in the 1970s?" "How can our congregation reach this community for Christ?" A creative Christian leader will use the panel discussion whenever basic information is needed to expose and discuss varying points of view on a contemporary issue.

9
Debates
Stimulate Interest

In his teen Sunday School class, Jim Murkhardt is attempting to deal with contemporary issues which relate to the lives of his students. In past weeks they have examined biblical positions on birth control, abortion, war, civil rights, the role of the church in contemporary society, and several other problems.

Next week the class will stage a debate. The question is whether Christian young people should attend Christian colleges or state schools. The issue has been structured into a positive proposition: "Resolved: Christian young people should attend Christian colleges." Tim and Cathy will be arguing the affirmative; Paul and Lois the negative. Each speaker has been assigned six minutes for his constructive speech and three minutes for rebuttal.

Since in a formal debate the affirmative always begins, Tim will speak first, followed by Lois, then Cathy, and finally, in the second negative slot, Paul will conclude the constructive speeches. Then, after approximately five minutes for the participants to work on their rebuttal thoughts, the order for the three-minute rebuttal speeches will be: Negative 1 — Lois; Affirmative 2 — Cathy; Negative 2 — Paul; and Affirmative 1 — Tim.

The burden of proof in a debate is on the affirmative unless the negative side offers an alternative proposal to the one resolved.

Paul and Lois will therefore try to counteract the seemingly good reasons for Christians to attend Christian schools. They do not have to prove that Christians should attend state schools, but only cast doubt on the validity of their attending Christian schools. There will be 10 or 15 minutes at the end for questions from the total group, but at that point Jim will be using a different teaching method called "forum," which will be discussed in a later chapter.

Although the procedure above sounds very formal, almost like parliamentary debate, keep in mind that this is a teaching-learning situation. While not really trying to prove that Christian students should attend Christian colleges, the plan is to get all of the arguments on the table so the class can see exactly what is involved in thinking through this very important issue.

In order to make the debate work, all of the participants must appear really convinced of their positions. It is possible that Paul and Lois already plan to attend a Christian college. But for purposes of the debate, they should seem thoroughly convinced of the negative side of the proposition.

Debate is simply a procedure in which two or more people compete in trying to persuade others to accept or reject a proposition as a foundation for belief or behavior. Although a form of discussion, it differs from discussion in several ways:

1. Debate is a presentation of the result rather than the airing of the process.
2. Debate is basically competitive whereas discussion should be cooperative.
3. Debate centers around an issue which is already defined, whereas a discussion generally is an attempt to delineate factors and define a position.

Values of Using Debate

Like other forms of discussion, debate offers a dialogical or participative approach to learning. Students actually have a significant role in the learning experiences. Debate also rests upon the firm principles of democratic procedure. Its very structure demonstrates that all positions should have an equal hearing and that truth can triumph over error even if error is convincingly presented.

Debate is also a time-saver. It might take twice the investment of time to air all of the issues which good debates will uncover in the 36 minutes of speaking time described above. The group can see the issues sharply drawn and the arguments logically presented on a controversial issue which may have been very cloudy in their thinking.

Perhaps the most significant benefit which will accrue from using debates in your classroom is the investment of preparation time by the participating students. Assigning the reading of a Bible chapter or the answering of five or six questions on an assignment sheet will not motivate a teenager like pitting him against two of his peers in open competition in the next class session will. Only the laziest of students would minimize his study in anticipation of such a dramatic event.

Debate involves great discipline. The need to not only research the facts but to present them in a coherent manner within a very limited time provides a definite challenge for the participants. The method teaches research, thinking, and speaking, as well as absorbing the subject matter under study.

Some students who may not find a role of service in the church or class through singing, songleading, or playing an instrument, may find themselves quite gifted in debate. Incidently, if you find success with the debating in your classroom, you may want to move to a larger group, presenting a formal debate on some crucial issue as a part of a Sunday evening service or other meeting to which the public would be invited.

Problems in the Debate Method

One of the major difficulties in structuring debates is the clarification of a good "resolved." The resolved should always be an affirmative statement presenting an issue which is clear not only to the debate participants, but also to the larger audience.

Speakers should be encouraged to attack the primary issues and not waste the limited time wandering down bypaths. Sometimes the abilities of members of opposing debate teams are inequitable, and the debate turns out to be a lopsided confrontation, an embarrassing experience for everyone involved. Divisiveness is always a danger, especially if the participants genuinely believe their positions and begin to attack each other during the session period. The teacher must guard against this.

Principles for Effective Use of Debates

Carefully *provide resources.* Probably debates could not be used effectively much below the teens, although an advanced junior high class might try some adapted versions. Without biasing the positions of the debaters, Jim will steer them to good sources (books, magazine articles, people) offering ammunition for the presentation. Jim will have to make sure that he gives both sides equally valuable resources and that he does not offer more help to one group than to the other.

The subject of the debate must be *controversial in nature.* It would be rather futile, for example, to argue the proposition, "Resolved: Murder should be illegal." Be careful not to allow the subject matter to become too technical or unrelated to the needs and interests of the members of your class.

In formal parliamentary debate, it is proper to take a vote from the assembly after the debaters have concluded to see which side won. That is probably *not* a good technique to use when you are employing the debate as a teaching method. The *object is to get the issues on the floor.* No doubt there will be a subjective decision formed in the minds of your students as to which side really presented the better argument. But there seems to be no value in embarrassing any of the participants by taking a win-lose vote.

There has to be *flexibility* on the part of the class and the teacher. If Jim is particularly biased toward the Christian college to the extent that he does not even want to hear the arguments against it, he would not be able to conduct a debate in his class properly. As mentioned earlier, the debate is clearly linked to the freedom-of-thought process which we treasure in our society and surely in our churches.

10
The Forum/Symposium as a Teaching Technique

Jim Murkhardt's class debate on Christian colleges was so successful that he is following it up with an open forum next week. Jim's denomination is having a Saturday evening youth fellowship hosted by his church, and one of the major features on the program is the presentation of the debate on Christian colleges, this time followed by a half hour *debate-forum*. When asked to handle this part of the program Jim was not sure whether he wanted to use a *forum*, a *colloquy*, or a *symposium*. Actually, he was not sure he understood the difference between those three techniques.

His pastor recommended that he check Martha Leypoldt's book, *40 Ways to Teach in Groups* (Judson, Valley Forge, Pa.), and there he found the following definitions:

Colloquy: Three or four persons selected from a group present various aspects of a problem to three or four resource persons who respond to them.

Debate Speakers who have opposing views on a contro-
Forum: versial subject are given equal time to present their reasons for their beliefs, followed by a

free and open discussion of the issue by the entire group.

Symposium: A series of speeches is given by as many speakers as there are aspects of a problem or issue.

Only the latter part of the second definition above applies to forum since the open discussion time which the term describes may follow any kind of presentation such as a debate, a sermon, a lecture, or even a story. All three approaches are much alike with the minor differences noted in the definitions above. The symposium differs from the panel in that the speakers do not discuss the subject among themselves. They make separate but related speeches (generally about 5 to 10 minutes in length). In order to have a genuine symposium, you must utilize both the formal speeches and the subsequent audience participation.

The colloquy (sometimes called "colloquium") differs from both the symposium and the forum in that there are two levels of participation: the one or two (usually not more than three) experts interact with other small groups of people. This might be the entire group if the class is small. On the other hand, this interaction may take place before a much larger audience so that really we have two groups of participants, the experts and the interacters.

Since Jim's objective for the presentation is to offer as much information as possible in a limited time, and to air two diverse points of view on an important subject, he could use standard debate, a symposium, a colloquy, or even a panel. Any of these could be followed by a forum to include questions and discussion from the larger group. Jim has chosen the debate-forum since his students already have the first part of that presentation prepared from their experience in class.

Values of the Forum Method
Since it is rarely used by itself, the forum should be viewed as a supplementary method which enhances and extends the benefits of other information-transmitting approaches to learning. It offers the additional dimension of allowing the audience to ask questions about points which were not clear during the previous presenta-

tion. The forum also provides an opportunity for the correcting of misimpressions given by the speakers. The forum is also a form of review in which the audience can again think through the issues, thereby providing additional order and design to the learning experience.

Good interest is usually maintained in a forum situation. When people hear controversial points of view presented by speakers or debaters, they tend to be drawn into the subject at hand and subsequently want to interact with the viewpoints of the speakers. Jim's major problem is limiting the questions and discussions to one half hour in view of the fact that the church expects over 100 young people to attend the youth fellowship.

The most significant person in the presentation will not be one of the experts. More important to the success of a forum is the chairman, who will keep the question on target, sort out key questions for discussion, prod the special speakers if necessary, and summarize the significant findings at the end of the session.

Jim is taking a chance in letting one of his teenagers handle the chairman's role. Larry is a sharp young fellow who is able to speak clearly and think alertly even while his attention is focused on another speaker. Without Larry, Jim would probably have chaired the forum himself. His choice is probably a wise one. If you have a young person who can handle the job, the value of involvement is worth the risk. If you seriously question the abilities of any potential chairman, play it safe and use an adult. The chairman's ability can be the difference between success and failure in a forum.

Problems in Using the Forum

The biggest danger in this teaching approach is failure to find an attractive subject. Sometimes a subject may be of interest to the speakers who live with its implications day by day but of little concern to the audience. If so, when time for questions is offered, everyone will sit silently looking at the chairman. Such an experience is embarrassing to the speakers, and deadly in terms of creating a vital learning experience. In thinking about using a forum for your class, make sure they all agree that the subject matter for discussion is relevant and meaningful to them.

Another problem is the danger of being overwhelmed by one

particular position. This is particularly dangerous when using a lecture-forum. It can also become a problem in debate, symposium, or colloquy if one side of the argument is weak. It is always difficult for a group to be objective on a controversial issue. But once a speaker has delineated an opinion and only one side of that issue has been adequately presented, it is almost impossible for an audience to consider the other side honestly and openly.

It is only fair to say also that using any teaching method of this kind takes time. The teacher who uses various forms of discussion will invariably be a teacher who is committed to quality rather than quantity. In other words, he is more interested that his students learn well the things which he presents than that they skim over a lot of material during the classtime.

Principles for Effective Use of the Forum

Remember the primary objective is to *stimulate thought* and offer information, not to solve problems.

Make sure the *chairman is competent* for his role, which includes introducing the speaker or speakers, reminding the audience to be ready to participate after the presentations are made, soliciting response from the larger group, clarifying questions and answers when necessary, avoiding awkward pauses of silence by posing questions himself, and keeping the discussion on the sharp edge of controversy. He must do all of this while refraining from a lengthy or prominent speaking role himself.

Make sure that the original presentations are as *objective and accurate* as possible. If misinformation is given during this stage of the method, the discussion will be an exploration in error and meaninglessness rather than truth.

Always *include a summary* at the conclusion which will attempt to clarify what issues have been presented, how they relate to one another, and what course of action should follow on the part of the group members.

11
Discovering
the Discovery Method

Too often Christian teachers behave as though authoritative truth has to be communicated in an authoritarian manner. In one sense, the attitude we have toward the Bible will largely determine how we teach it. But our ultimate purpose is to get students to be independent investigators of God's Word forming firsthand standards and convictions which are taught them by the Holy Spirit. In order to accomplish this purpose, it would seem that our teaching should reflect the fact that infallible truth is nevertheless being handled by fallible teachers.

If we can recognize this about ourselves, then perhaps we can experiment with the discovery method. Discovery teaching (sometimes called the "inquiry method") is simply the process of allowing the student to take the leading role in his own learning experiences. The teacher becomes a facilitator and guide, making it possible for the learner to reach mutually-agreed-upon goals. The teacher serves as a resource person to stimulate, motivate, clarify, and explain.

The atmosphere in which such teaching takes place must be informal and nonthreatening. In order for discovery teaching to be effective, the environment (including the teacher's attitude) must *contribute to* rather than *detract from* the attaining of objectives.

Rather than forcing his idea of content, the teacher attempts to keep his hands off the learning process whenever and wherever the student can carry it on for himself.

Such a free-rein approach to education is threatening to some teachers. The instructor who considers himself an indispensable purveyor of information about God may find it very difficult to play down his role in order to maximize student involvement. Some concepts of education largely involve lectures and drills, and center almost exclusively on the teacher's performance during class. Paul Pallmeyer questions such an attitude about Christian teaching when he asks, "Is such teaching likely to produce the kind of thinking a Christian needs to do for his own faith in the complex life of today — and tomorrow? Or a prior question: Is it information we are trying to communicate or is it the Christian faith? The two are not necessarily the same. In fact, the way we arrive at the information may have as much to do with the kind of faith that results (or doesn't result) as the information itself" (*New Ways to Learn,* Dale E. Griffin, ed.; Concordia, St. Louis, Mo.).

Discovery teaching brings four basic components of the educational setting into interaction: the student, the teacher, the environment, and the content. The *student* is an active participant who solves problems which he understands through the process of structuring his own learning experiences. The *teacher* plays the role of resource person, as described above. The *environment* includes both freedom and structure with freedom having the upper hand. The *content* may very well be propositional truth in a general context, waiting in the proper place for the student to track it down, confront it, and capture it for his own.

An effective discovery leader must be a mature teacher who knows not only the subject matter of the current lesson, but has a depth understanding of Christian truth. Specific objectives may not guarantee that learning time will be well spent, but they certainly facilitate that desirable goal. The student has to be a willing participant, ready to explore numerous avenues of information, aggressively ready to appropriate new findings in the light of previous information and a total biblical world view. What he gets will be his own and will therefore fit his needs and interests. He will not wander around in theological Saul's armor, as so many contemporary Christian teenagers do, when he marches forth to fight the Goliaths of a pagan society.

Values of Discovery Teaching
Discovery teaching allows for individualistic accomplishments. It is highly adaptive and versatile, limited only by the imagination of the participants at both the teacher and student level. The bugaboos of boredom and apathy should be reduced to a minimum since total student participation and self-direction is necessary. This inquiry method allows for free expression of individual creativity. It is a concept of learning about which we talk much and do little.

The relationship of students to teachers and of students to students should develop rapidly and warmly in the inquiry approach. Group activity is significant, and the sharing of findings is the end result of individual initiative. Actually a number of diverse methods can be used within the framework of discovery learning, since any single student may approach his subject matter from different perspectives. Surely, numerous different approaches will be adopted within the total group.

Problems in Discovery Teaching
Many students feel insecure in an unstructured environment of learning. It is much more comfortable to be able to listen to a lecture and take notes in orderly fashion than to be confronted with the haunting question, "What do you want to learn about this subject, and how do you propose to learn it?"

Any time there is freedom in education, there is also responsibility. If that responsibility is not taken seriously by the participants, the whole process could get out of control. This freedom can also threaten the organization because a given class might decide that they could accomplish their purposes better by meeting at a different hour, in a different place, or on a different day than that class is usually scheduled.

The inquiry method is also time-consuming. At times a student will pursue a subject for a while, only to wander down some fruitless bypaths. Nevertheless, the very frustration of the search is a learning experience. One of the things that all of us have to understand in the process of education is where *not* to look for certain kinds of information.

Perhaps the most crucial problem of discovery teaching is the tendency to slip away from propositional revelation. From a Christian point of view, the inquiry method is *not* matching interviews, library reference research, brainstorming, discussion, and Bible study as equal approaches to truth. It is rather viewing the Scripture as a very fine mesh at the tube end of a funnel. All of the sources are poured into the wide mouth at the top, but *only what filters through the screen of divine revelation can in the final analysis be considered truth.*

Principles for Effective Teaching by Discovery

In the helpful little paperback mentioned previously, Pallmeyer suggests that Christian teachers ought to do two things for their students: *encourage the questioning mind,* and *equip students with skills* for finding the answers. He goes on to say, "We can do both by using Inquiry Method — presenting pupils with problems and putting them to work finding the solutions by whatever means available. We may suggest resources, but we need to refrain from doing the research *for* the learner. To train our students to think, we must also challenge the answers they suggest and not be satisfied with the easy answer they are 'supposed to get.' We must require our pupils to give evidence and make a convincing case for what they think and say."

In a very real sense the inquiry method is a matter of *confrontation.* The teacher confronts the student with issues which have meaning and relevance for him, with freedom to pursue those issues, or the problems which stand in the way of solving the issues, and with the resources through which and from which answers can be found.

Those *resources have to be available and usable* by the student. It does no good, for example, to send a high school student to a Greek concordance for a word study on *sanctification.* The student also needs to be taught how to use the resources as he tracks his solutions through books, articles, films, recordings, maps, experiences, projects, and most important, other people.

Perhaps the most productive results of discovery teaching will take place in groups of adolescents and adults, although classes of advanced Juniors might very well pursue a scaled-down version of the inquiry method. A certain amount of *maturity is necessary* since an individual must be aware of his own feelings and opinions to be adequately involved in problem-solving techniques. If we expect the Word of God to produce growth in the lives of students, they must be involved directly with its text, and this is precisely what happens in effective discovery teaching.

12
Using Projects in Teaching

An old Chinese proverb states:

> I hear and I forget,
> I see and I remember,
> I do and I understand.

Katherine Tobey stresses the validity of the project method when she says, "Only in the *act of doing* does one discover that the process is more important than the product. It is in the process that the learning takes place. Having had their own experiences in creative expression, adults become more sensitive teachers and more well-rounded persons" (*Learning and Teaching Through the Senses,* Westminster Press, Philadelphia, Pa.).

Projects may take various forms and shapes. When a given project closely approximates the activity for which a class is preparing the student, the value of learning by doing makes this method an extremely significant one.

Consider, for example, the matter of preparing college students to be elementary teachers. The project method is frequently used in education classes in colleges and universities because it has the value of bringing the student into touch with a bit of reality. Education majors prepare picture files, develop entire units of work in social studies or science, and work through case studies on imaginary or real children.

The ultimate project is student teaching experience in which the college student spends time observing, then helping, finally actually teaching in a live situation. In seminary education this is called "internship," as a young man serves for a period of time under the supervision of a mature pastor who is able to help him experience realistic tasks and responsibilities of pastoral ministry.

But this dimension is beyond our use in the classroom. We will be concerned with small projects, most of which take perhaps only one week and usually not more than two or three months. Findley Edge divides projects into four categories: information, attitude, habit, and service. A good example of *information projects* would be research and reports assigned in an adult Sunday School class. *Attitude projects* could be implemented through surveys and interviews, probably culminating in a report of some kind. For his examples of a *habit project,* Edge lists daily Bible reading, regular attendance at church services, or the initiation of family worship. *Service projects* are perhaps the most familiar to us as they take form in Gospel teams, visitation, work projects around the church, or fund raising for some specific goal (*Helping the Teacher,* Broadman Press, Nashville, Tenn.).

My former colleague, Professor Elmer Towns, had an interesting way of describing the variations in the project method by suggesting the following five unit breakdown of types:

1. Search-out-the-experience-of-others project. Illustration: read about others who baptized
2. Seek-the-factors-of-an-experience project. Illustration: analyze the steps of baptizing
3. Recreate-the-experience project. Illustration: diagram a specific baptizing situation
4. Observe-the-experience project. Illustration: watch a baptism
5. Go-through-the-experience project. Illustration: baptize someone

Values in the Project Method
Projects introduce the dimension of fun into learning. This is im-

portant not only in teaching children but facilitates education at all age levels. Not all projects are fun, but the dimension of interest is certainly heightened when student involvement on a realistic and experiential plane is set into motion.

Another value of the project approach is that it has a number of fringe benefits. Let us go back to the student teacher. Primarily she is learning how to teach the various subjects in a self-contained classroom at the third grade level. At the same time, however, she is learning how to make out reports, keep a disciplined schedule of employment, get along with other people, and operate in a defined system of evaluation. None of these may be overt objectives of the experience, but almost all of them will accrue to the benefit of the participant.

Remember that the project has two dimensions: the learning process which results from the participation, and the end result which has value to the class and/or other people. When the junior high class goes visiting in the senior citizens home, the class learns about witness and sharing with others, and the elderly folks benefit from their visit and the inspiration the young people bring them.

Problems in the Project Method

Generally speaking, a project will take some kind of materials. If the project is geared to information gathering, some books or people must be available for that resource. If the project is one of service, it may require paint, wood, or perhaps instruments, or transportation to the senior citizens home. Most of the time it is possible to procure these materials, and the teacher should not consider this a major drawback.

Sometimes the project becomes an end in itself, and we forget that it is primarily a teaching technique. As a technique, it must be closely related to the unit of study in which the class is engaged. The project should be determined by the *objectives* of the class rather than having the unit of study governed by what available projects are at hand.

As with other good methods which stress student involvement, the project takes time. Sometimes students tire of the project experience before it is finished, and the loss of interest bogs it down in the final lap. Because of this problem, teachers should be careful to select projects of length adapted to the ages and interests of a given class.

In *Creative Teaching in the Church,* Eleanor Morrison and Virgil Foster describe a junior high class which took on a twofold project geared to portray the disciples' role in the last events of the life of our Lord. They wrote a radio script on the pattern of the CBS television program "You Are There" and prepared a large wall mural in conjunction with the study. The entire project took over six weeks, with small groups working on various phases of the two projects. The authors describe a secret of success in this approach: "Young people are most likely to be interested when each one has a free choice of the group with which he wishes to work. Also . . . working on a concrete project with one's hands, along with the study, created more interest than discussion alone" (Prentice-Hall, Englewood Cliffs, N.J.).

Principles for Effective Use of the Project Method

Preparation is the key, and it should include discussing the objectives of the project and securing the participation of the group at the planning stage. Students should be involved in deciding what form the project should take as well as carrying out the specifics of getting the job done. Actually the plan is very important because in this phase the class comes to grips with such significant factors as the duration of the project, its cost, the extent of its impact on other people, and how it will be evaluated.

In carrying out the project the teacher is an ever-present source of *encouragement and resource*. Without pushing the students unduly, he keeps them on target and reminds them of deadline dates which they themselves approved in the planning stage. The enthusiastic support of the class is necessary to carry a project through the implementation phase.

Perhaps the project will be done outside of class entirely. If that is the case, *set aside classtime* for questions, progress reports, and modification of plans.

The third phase leads us to another principle. *Evaluation* is necessary if the project is going to be a genuine learning experience. The class and the teacher together will decide whether the project was successful, whether it accomplished the goals set for it, what areas were deficient, and what should be changed if it is ever used again. Each student should be encouraged to specify what values the learning experience had for him.

Properly used, the project method can bring new life into a class which has become bogged down with nonparticipating methodology or perhaps has even stagnated on overuse of some discussion technique. Think through your next year of teaching. How can you effectively use projects with your students?

13
Instructive Play as Learning

During the historical period of the Napoleonic wars, a young educator rose to prominence in Germany who was to have a profound impact on the future of education, even up to the present day. Friedrich Froebel was born in 1782 into the home of a pastor. His mother died when he was only nine months old, and he never enjoyed warm relations with his stepmother, a situation which seems to have had significant influence on his educational thought.

His educational ideas centered on the cultivation of awareness, love, and independence, and he once wrote, "The aim and object of parental care, in the domestic and family circle, is to awaken and develop, to quicken all the powers and natural gifts of the child, to enable all the members and organs of man to fulfill the requirements of the child's powers and gifts. The natural mother does all of this instinctively, without instruction and direction; but this is not enough: it is needful that she should do it consciously" (*The Education of Man,* Augustus M. Kelley Publishers, Clifton, N.J.).

Along with one of his contemporaries, Johann Pestalozzi, Froebel developed a concept of education which promoted the validity of games and fun as a significant part of the educational process. In the book mentioned above Froebel wrote, "A child that plays thoroughly, with self-active determination, perseveringly until physical fatigue forbids, will surely be a thorough, determined man, capable of self-sacrifice for the promotion of the welfare of himself and others."

Froebel's view emerged from his focus on creativity and freedom in man. He was no Christian in the sense that we would use that term, but he certainly understood the nature of the universe as a gigantic object lesson developed by the creative hand of God, and he wanted to pattern his educational practices after that kind of example.

Many adults think that the early childhood departments of both public and Christian education have too much emphasis on play. In many cases such a criticism may be warranted. But there are two polar misunderstandings here which lead to a confusion of this teaching method. The first misunderstanding is a failure to recognize the significance of play activities in the educational process. The old puritanical idea that any kind of study is good as long as all of it is hard and some of it is unpleasant has been discounted long ago by competent educators. This is not to assert that discipline is not desirable in the educational process, but to state categorically that difficulty does not insure learning.

The other problem stems from a failure on the part of some teachers to make classroom play and games genuinely *instructive*. Almost all toys and play activities should be educational to some extent. They should be promoting the physical, mental, emotional, social, and spiritual maturation of the child. Eleanor Morrison and Virgil Foster wrote, "Play is the business of small children. Through play they find out about their world and how to relate to other persons. In play they express their feelings and ideas. In play they try on what it is like to be another person" (*Creative Teaching in the Church,* mentioned earlier).

No doubt a number of categories of instructive play could be developed, but let me suggest four to help us organize our thinking:
1. *Educational Toys.* In this category we would include blocks, books, clay, dolls, paste, paint, crayons, and other things which the children would use in creative play in an elementary classroom. Blocks, for example, could be used to build a church or a home after the children have heard a story about

God's house or about their parents and how children are loved and wanted. Sharing the blocks is as important an experience for Billy as thinking about the little church he is building. The preschool child is learning to be a part of a group larger than his own family.

2. *Music.* Although we will deal with music instruction in a different chapter, it deserves mention here because of the use of motion choruses, group singing, rhythm bands, and other dramatic expression which is definitely instructive play.

3. *Finger plays.* Children can act out verses and rhythms with their fingers, either in connection with music or in relation to some story.

4. *Puzzles and Contests.* Instructive play can leave the Nursery and Preschool rooms and move all the way up into the High School Department. Sword drills, Bible quizzes, crossword puzzles, and other forms of games are a deliberate attempt to teach biblical content through a fun approach to education.

One of the newest and most significant processes used today in the training of executives and administrators is called "Simulation Gaming." Gaming approaches are used to change attitudes and develop personality. Such an objective is not far removed from what we are trying to do through instructive play in the Kindergarten room.

Values in Instructive Play

One of the most significant values of educational games in teaching small children is the opportunity which they afford the teacher to observe the child in a natural situation. When a child is caught up in a game, he tends to forget that an authority figure is present. As a result deficiencies of attitude and human behavior quickly emerge. Thus, the teacher or parent can see them and deal with them.

To quote Morrison and Foster again, "If the children are only talked to, or participate only in activities directed by a teacher, it is difficult for a teacher to know at what point each child is or is not growing in his ability to understand, trust, and love others. It is in the spontaneous interactions of children that a listening, sensitive teacher can find out what progress is being made by a child in living religiously with others."

Another obvious value of this approach to the teaching-learning process is the enthusiastic involvement which it generally elicits from the student. No really effective teacher enjoys "making" a child learn. Teaching becomes a joy when children enter willingly and joyfully into the educational activities which we have planned for them. If those educational activities take the form of play, that positive reaction will be gained much more quickly.

Sometimes instructive play results from a carefully planned design set up by the teacher in advance. Other times the children will themselves gravitate toward the kind of play that represents recent environmental influences or interests. When my family and I were on a world trip in 1972, we cleared customs inspection in 17 countries. About half way through the trip we looked in on our children one day to find them busily playing customs inspector, with one rummaging through the suitcase of another. We had not taught them the game. Their own creative resources had produced it out of the fabric of their own experiences. Because of its inhibition-releasing form, instructive play does help develop creativity in our students.

Paul Torrance writes that "curiosity, the instinct of play, the instinct to manipulate, and the like have been suggested as natural guides to learning. Educational innovators such as Pestalozzi, Froebel, Binet, Montessori, and others made use of these forces, but recognized clearly that curiosity, playfulness, and manipulativeness unguided cannot be depended upon to bring about learning" (*Encouraging Creativity in the Classroom,* W. C. Brown and Co., Dubuque, Iowa).

Problems in Teaching Through Instructive Play

As suggested earlier, the inherent weakness in the system is that play will cease to be instructive. At all levels of education there is so much to be learned, and seemingly so little time to learn it, that the sincere teacher dare not allow time to be wasted. Particularly in Christian education, where what we have to communicate is so crucial because of its eternal nature, we want to be sure that every activity of the classroom, formal or informal, leads toward the accomplishment of worthy objectives.

Other less significant dangers could be mentioned. A playtime situation might get out of hand when directed by a teacher with minimal discipline skills. Proper equipment is needed, and a cost is involved in its purchase. In the final analysis, however, the virtues of instructive play will greatly overbalance the pitfalls if the teacher can keep his eye on the fulfillment of learning goals.

Principles for Effective Use of Instructive Play

The wise teacher will want to allow sufficient *freedom and flexibility* in the play process for children to find their own way in certain things. For example, in the modeling of clay, if the children are told to "make a cross," they will either attempt to make it as much like the teacher's model as possible or ask the teacher to make it for them so they will not have an inferior production. If, on the other hand, they are given a lump of clay and asked to make something that would help to remind them of Jesus our Saviour, a variety of symbols and ideas might result from the creative powers of the children's minds.

With respect to the use of play that is genuinely instructive, the following list of *evaluative questions* will be helpful in looking back on the classroom experience in which we have used this method:

1. Was it enjoyable to all of the students?
2. Were new skills developed during the classroom period?
3. After the game, was group discussion well used?
4. Did the play seem to increase social cooperative behavior?
5. Were the children too dependent on their teacher during the playtime?
6. Did the game so excite the children that they could not settle down for the next aspect of the classtime?
7. Was the game genuinely purposeful, or was it just filler?
8. If we used this game before, did the children show genuine improvement this time?

If you have not used instructive play or educational games before, you might want to visit a Christian bookstore in your town and look at some of the materials available. You will find everything from toys for small nursery children to rather complex and difficult Bible games for advanced teens and adults. Everyone loves to play, and, if he can make play a learning experience, the creative teacher will be excited about the results.

14
Field Trips
in Church Education

One of the most popular educational models has surfaced in the past two decades in Edgar Dale's "Cone of Experience." Since first appearing in his book *Audiovisual Methods in Teaching* (Holt, Rinehart, and Winston, New York, N.Y.), it has been reprinted in numerous books on teaching process and used thousands of times in educational classrooms. (See page 79.)

Notice how Dale places field trips in the middle of the cone but closer to the level of "Direct, purposeful experiences" than to the extreme abstraction at the top. Dale would argue that too much education takes place at the top where we merely exchange verbal or visual symbols rather than getting down to "gut level" things that actually make up realistic life experiences.

Taking a field trip to a Jewish synagogue is not the same as attending rabbinical school for several years. But it will give teens studying modern Judaism a considerably better view of what is actually going on in the currect practice of that faith than reading the chapter about it in the handbook, or listening to a teacher's lecture.

In her book *40 Ways to Teach in Groups* (mentioned earlier), Martha Leypoldt refers to three steps in the leader's responsibility in field trip education: *preparation, at the place,* and *evaluation.*

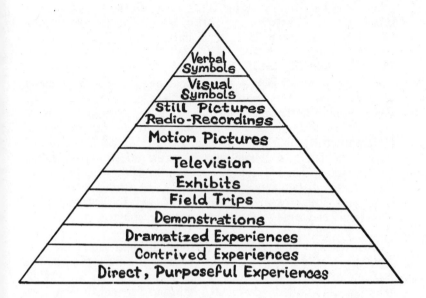

In preparation for the trip the leader,
1. Makes all preliminary arrangements with the person(s) in charge of the place to be visited
2 Describes the purpose of the proposed visit
3. Presents relevant data regarding the place to be visited
4. Presents instructions regarding transportation to the place of interest and decorum to be observed while there

The example of Christ in taking His disciples to the places of action was a very positive demonstration of "learning by doing." They went to the Temple, to the seaside, to the desert, and to various villages to minister, but also to learn the many wonderful things which the Master had to teach them. We can follow His example today by taking our students "where the action is" to observe firsthand the people or practices about which we are teaching. Wayne R. Rood suggests that "The undebatable effectiveness of learning by doing is due to the fact that data and skills are acquired by total involvement. Lessons are not learned by the mind alone but literally by the whole body, all the senses, the entire experience. Facts become part of life" (*The Art of Teaching Christianity,* Abingdon Press, Nashville, Tenn.).

Values of Field Trip Teaching

The purpose of a field trip is to expose our students to firsthand experiences with people, places, or things. In the case of the earlier example, the obvious value is that being in the synagogue brings the students closer to reality. It also introduces that all-important learning dimension, interest.

A good field trip should also have the effect of stimulating further study. The students not only observe the situation while they are there, but are encouraged to think further about what they have seen. Many teachers work hard to develop "post-classroom carry over." The field trip has this ingredient built into it from the start.

There is also an element of personal involvement in the field trip, particularly if the teacher has been wise enough to allow the students to participate actively in the planning of the trip. While they are on location, touring the site and listening to the local leaders, students are co-learners with their teacher and are therefore experiencing an independence from him which is healthy in developing their own learning potential.

Field trips are not limited to any particular age group. In fact, they tend to work very well with small children as well as advanced teens and adults.

Older students need to learn the reality of "the fellowship of learning." Christian people in interaction with one another can be engaged in a warm atmosphere of mutual sharing in cooperation with the Holy Spirit's supernatural teaching. Paul Lederach reminds us that "the impact and influence of class members on each other provide powerful forces for supporting learning. Effective teaching requires that the group be involved" (*Learning to Teach,* Herald Press, Scottdale, Pa.). Field trip education gives us an opportunity to exhibit such open situation learning as a witness to the unity of the Church in Christ.

Problems in Field Trip Education

Rood mentions one of the common pitfalls into which many

teachers unconsciously fall when centering on activity education: "It is easy for a teacher so to succumb to the activity method that he will place excessive emphasis on sharing activity, letting it become an end in itself. Moving about does not necessarily develop the mind or the spirit." As in all other methods, the field trip must lead toward the achieving of clear-cut learning objectives which have been set for the class.

Some churches face the problem of limited resources because of their locations. Sometimes however, substitutes can be found. For example, if it is impossible to visit a Jewish synagogue as mentioned earlier, the class studying the habits and customs of contemporary Judaism might at least find a Jewish family nearby and plan a visit to their home.

A more common problem than limited resources is the failure on the part of many of us to recognize the value of the resources we have. You might want to take 15 or 20 minutes after you have finished reading this chapter just to brainstorm the potential within 20 or 30 minutes driving time from your church. Are there any sites of historical significance? How about noted churches or other buildings?

Katherine Tobey encourages trips to visit the mission work of the church and says, "Young people studying some of the social problems faced by the church are eager to glimpse firsthand the work being done in depressed areas both in the large cities and mixed ethnic populations, and in the isolated rural areas. This interest makes it possible for church leaders to arrange chartered bus tours to mission centers during the summer vacations. When a person actually sees how the church is meeting personal needs, then he is more eager to help" (*Learning and Teaching Through the Senses*, mentioned earlier).

Lack of preparation can be a real problem too. Students should know what to expect and what to look for when they visit a site. You might even prepare questions in advance to be answered while the students are touring or immediately upon returning from the trip.

Principles for Effective Use of Field Trips

Involve students in planning the trip from the start. Before the trip the students should read about the place to be visited and make preparations for the trip as suggested by the leader.

Keep the group small. If your class is unusually large, you may have to divide them into subgroups and have several trips or different sections or platoons, each with its own leader who can guide the learning activities on location. Not only is this valid for educational purposes, it also saves wear and tear on the teacher that would result from too large a group.

Select wise trip times. Be sure the group agrees to take the trip before embarking on it. Otherwise members will not be as open to learning from the trip and may even forget to come that day.

Plan evaluation sessions after the trip. This session may be an informal discussion time at the site or back in the classroom. Or, it may take the form of a written test to check the impressions and intake of the students.

Plan now to include a field trip in your teaching program for the next quarter. It will increase the learning of your class and be fun too.

15
Teaching
for Memorization

All of us want to think that we are biblical in our teaching methodology since we recognize that the Word of God is not only the
foundation for the content that we teach, but also our example
for technique. Almost every book on teaching emphasizes the
dialogue approach, which Jesus frequently used, and urges the
participation method, based on His example. Such an emphasis
is correct, but sometimes we forget the great heritage which the
Old Testament Jewish faith provides for Christian education. The
focus on the family, the centricity of Scripture in all learning, and
the later commitment to quality learning in the synagogue schools
are all worthy of our study. The one teaching methodology
which reigned supreme throughout all of those Old Testament cen-
turies was catechism, or memorization.

In his *History of Christian Education,* C. B. Eavey tells us of the
mnemonic drill which took place at home from the earliest years
of the child's life. "As soon as he was able to speak, his parents
began to teach him words and sentences. The first memory tasks
were mainly blessings, especially those that formed part of the
daily prayers. The child rose from bed with one of these upon his
lips and went to bed reciting words proclaiming belief in the one
God. Much stress was placed upon memorization. As he grew

older, he was required to memorize portions of the Scriptures. The mother had a large part in the training of the earliest years, but it was considered the duty of the father to assume responsibility for directing this more advanced phase of the child's education" (Moody Press, Chicago, Ill.).

Memorization may be defined simply as the power, function, or act of reproducing and identifying what has been heard or experienced. It has been suggested that there are at least four steps in the memory process:

1. *Impression* — the original, conscious, meaningful experience itself
2. *Retention* — the process by which the experience is retained in the mind
3. *Recall* — the act of calling upon the mind for certain needed past experiences or ideas
4. *Recognition* — the recalled memory as an experience which the individual has had previously

Not all memorization is of the kind that we have come to call "rote." Rote memory describes the exact reproduction of past experiences, such as the memorization of a verse of Scripture which a student has learned. It is perfectly legitimate, however, to use memorization of general content and context of information as an approach to teaching. For example, one might memorize the general theme of each chapter in the Book of Acts although none of his reproduced content is exactly in the words of the text itself.

Values of Memorization Teaching

Memorization can be enjoyable for students. Too often we think of it only as a regular discipline which requires concentration and drill. But there is intrinsic motivation and instant reinforcement in the child's learning program when he realizes that he can accurately reproduce information which he has studied. Incidentally, one of the most popular types of adult classes in some Sunday Schools recently is the Bible memory class.

Although a valid end in itself, the memorization of Scripture and other valuable Christian truth is also an important means to other ends. For example, one's teaching of others is greatly facilitated by the content he has memorized as a student. Personal witnessing will be enhanced by one's ability to plug in important passages of Scripture to support and strengthen his case for the Gospel.

Some educators would argue that the very process of discipline in memorization is a valid and important technique. It is mind training of the highest order and will develop proficiency which is applicable in the entire development of one's educational pattern.

God has promised us that there is an inherent spiritual value in memorization of Scripture. David once wrote, "Thy Word have I hid in mine heart, that I might not sin against Thee" (Ps. 119: 11). Although later subconscious recall is certainly not the first aim of Scripture memorization, many young people and adults who were trained in the memorization of God's truth while children, later came to a real awakening of spiritual values because of that vital information hidden in their hearts.

Problems in Memorization Teaching

A constantly hovering cloud over memorization teaching is the possibility of *substituting words for meaning*. Sometimes children reciting memory verses seem too much like the trained seal who has been conditioned to bounce a rubber ball on his nose. They become performers whose striking ability is fascinating to the audience but has little inherent value or understanding to the performer.

Of course this does not have to be the case. Those of us who take a serious view of the inspiration and authority of the Bible will always be concerned that the experiences which a child has teach him the *meaning* of God's truth, but that meaning is inherent in the *words* of God's truth. However, the extraction of the meaning from the word is not always automatic. That is where the role of the teacher comes in.

Eleanor Morrison and Virgil Foster, in their book *Creative Teaching in the Church* (mentioned earlier), suggest that the child experiences God's truth even before its words have much meaning for him. "The ground for teaching and learning is in present experiences. This is true of all ages, but especially so of pre-school children. We do not, therefore, teach preschoolers many of the words of the Bible, which are beyond their comprehension. We attempt to provide experiences for which they know that love and forgiveness which are a part of God's word to man. Since the deepest experiences of life are often beyond words, the challenge to the preschool teacher is to act out the Christian Gospel."

I suspect that you and I might want to pay more attention to the text of Scripture than do the authors of this book. Nevertheless, what they suggest is essentially correct. The experiences which a child has (for that matter, the experiences of teens and adults as well) support or reject the essence of the word we are trying to teach. His confrontation with the *words* of Scripture is made meaningful by his confrontation with the *Word* as lived and shown to him by his parents and teachers.

Another problem with memorization teaching is that sometimes the process can become dull. I have already suggested that it does not have to be so, for memorization can be interesting, even exciting. But if we "sell" the technique as a hardship instead of a blessing, as a discipline instead of a delight, we build in negative attitudinal responses when we want precisely the reverse. Of course, the responses we get in any kind of teaching are determined largely by the way the presentation is made.

We have come a long way from the New England primer stuffed down the throats of reticent pupils by a stern schoolmaster with a stick. Or at least we *should* have come a long way from those days when learning was seen to be a necessary evil. Let us show our students — children, youth, or adults — that learning is the mother of many of the happy experiences of life, and that memorization is one of her happy children.

Principles for Effective Memorization

In order to make memorization a pleasant and productive skill, try to follow these guidelines when employing this teaching technique:

Remember that the memorization of *general content* can be as important and valuable a learning experience as rote memorization.

Master all the memorization which you require of your students.

Use helpful visual aids in teaching memory work. These will include pictures, flash cards, chalkboard, flannelgraph, and various kinds of projection.

Remember that *review* is the key to retention. Your students may memorize information and then forget it days or weeks later unless you subject them to frequent recall.

Always *emphasize understandings and meanings.* Do not let students of any age memorize just for the sake of performance, but make sure they understand the significance the learning has in their own lives.

16
Research
and Reports

Very few Sunday School teachers are content with the studying their students do outside the classroom. Surely a very small percentage of all Sunday School students in evangelical churches even bother to do the home study lessons in their manuals. Those who go beyond that elementary stage to any kind of depth study on a biblical topic are as hard to find as a Sunday School teacher who studies next week's lesson on Monday!

There are a number of ways to secure this home study, and we will talk about more of them in a future chapter dealing with the use of assignments in church education. In these present paragraphs we want to narrow our attention to a focus on the use of research and reports as a teaching technique. Our approach centers almost exclusively on preclass preparation rather than carry-over technique. To put it another way, the student will benefit more strategically from home study which he does on a subject to be discussed in the next class session, rather than review of last week's class. The value then comes not only in the process of home study itself, but also in the input which he is able to provide for the discussion time in the class session.

It would seem that this method would be most commonly employed in teaching teens or adults. No doubt its great validity on that level should make it a popular choice in those departments. But we must not let the awesome scholarly overtones of the word *research* frighten us away from using this technique with older children and young teens as well. The acceleration of home study programs and the use of library and learning resource center materials in public education today have prepared most late Primary, Junior, and Junior High students to engage in serious individualized study outside of a collective classroom setting.

Values of Research and Report Teaching
Chapter 11 dealt with an approach to learning which is presently called the "discovery method" or "inquiry learning." If we accept the basic principles of the inquiry approach, then one of our most significant purposes is making our students independent investigators of God's truth. This cannot be done simply by the transmissive pouring-out of information about God's truth. It requires rather that the student enter a firsthand confrontation with the facts. Paul Pallmeyer writes, "In giving pupils the task of finding their answers also to the religious questions of life, a teacher can employ or suggest a variety of techniques: interviews with schoolmates, teachers, parents, and other people in the community; reflective thinking; group discussions; reading; individual or group research and reports; etc. In the use of the inquiry method our role as teacher is that of a research director and advisor to those engaged in the study" (*New Ways to Learn,* see p. 65).

Another purposeful result of the use of research and reports is increased learning on the part of the teacher. Too infrequently we think of ourselves as co-learners with our students. This is particularly a problem in monological teaching in which the teacher becomes a purveyor of information, a large pitcher pouring facts into the gathered cups.

When our students are engaged in research, they are frequently being confronted with diverse ideas and new positions. As they make their reports, these positions are aired in class and helpful discussion can follow. If our preparation for this discussion is sufficiently thorough, we are experiencing this exposure with our students. That is good for us. It also forces us to stabilize our own positions and come up with better support for the things we say in class.

Research and reports actually extend the teaching time. If our students pay attention to the subject matter only during the class hour, then we have confronted them with "the lesson" for approximately 45 minutes per week. If, on the other hand, their exposure to the content of what we are trying to teach extends to another two or three hours in preparation for next week's class, then we have tripled or perhaps even quadrupled the exposure time, and that is a gold mine in which any teacher should want to be digging.

Problems in the Use of Research and Reports

In any kind of human endeavor, the worker does what the boss *inspects* and not what he *expects*. If we are going to make research assignments meaningful, that research must find its culmination in reports, and that takes classtime. This is a "difficulty" because many teachers feel compulsive pressure to present a certain amount of material just because the manual calls for a lesson on six chapters in 1 Kings this Sunday.

If student Jim is going to spend two or three hours in research during this week, we are going to have to let him have a segment of classtime to report on his research. Consequently we are going to cover less ground in a given amount of time. But the depth learning which will accrue is many times more valuable than the elementary overview which we too often settle for in Christian teaching.

Another common problem in the use of research reports is motivation. Sometimes extrinsic motivation such as awards and rewards may be necessary to get a class moving. But we want to work toward the goal of intrinsic motivation in which the excitement of the very learning itself will be its own reward. Obviously this kind of goal is more easily reached with advanced teens and adults than with children. The key is the kind of attitude which we develop in class toward the research both when it is assigned and when it is reported.

Principles of Effective Research Teaching

Martha Leypoldt (*40 Ways to Teach in Groups,* mentioned earlier) suggests that in research and report teaching there are 9 responsibilities of the class leader and 11 responsibilities of group members. The following lists are reproduced from pages 96 to 97 in her book:

The leader
  1. Assists in selecting a problem or issue
  2. Leads the group in determining the needed area of research on the topic
  3. Requests group members to volunteer to do research on the specific aspects determined by the group
  4. Suggests possible resources, or provides the resources for group members to use for the research
  5. Asks for reports from the individuals at the subsequent meeting
  6. Requests reactions from other group members to the reports
  7. Summarizes the main points, or requests someone else to do this task
  8. Suggests a course of action or a way to use the information
  9. Evaluates the group's learning experience

The group members
  1. Assist in selecting a problem or issue facing them
  2. Assist the leader in determining the needed areas of research on the topic
  3. Volunteer to do research on specific areas
  4. Use the resources suggested by the leader and search for additional resources
  5. Study diligently on the specific assignment given
  6. Select relevant data
  7. Organize material to present to the group
  8. Report findings of their research
  9. Ask questions of other group members to clarify issues
  10. Determine a course of action or way to use the information
  11. Assist in evaluating the group's learning experience

If you have not implemented this method in your class before, you may want to begin with short and specific research assignments. The less experienced the researcher, the more both the task and resources will have to be spelled out for him. But give it a try. Maybe you can use a verse which has several seemingly valid interpretations. The class (or individual class members) can interview Bible teachers, check commentaries, or track down cross-references to clarify the possible meanings and rate the one they consider most accurate. Soon you will discover that research and reports are tools for individual learning.

17
Teaching
Through Music

The basic joy of Christian faith makes music a learning ingredient even more important in Christian education than it is in secular education. The status of music as a universal language offers an outstanding vehicle for the communication of any message, and more particularly, for the message of the eternal Gospel. Lawrence Bixler says that this universal language appeals first to the emotions and then to the intellect. The emotions serve as a doorway to the throne room of the mind.

"Christian education must be concerned with the whole person, that is, emotions as well as intellect. Music is important to Christian education because of its appeal to the whole person. In its appeal it begins with the emotions or the moods and extends to the whole spirit of man" (*How To Teach,* Standard Publishing, Cincinnati, Ohio).

For too long the evangelical church has considered music only filler. The church has failed to take seriously its important responsibility in music education. Since Christian music is distinctly related to the church, the total task of church education includes confronting children, youth, and adults with the best of Christian music, and training those who possess talent to use it for Christ.

Of course this raises the question, "What is good church music?" Gunner Urang's book *Church Music for the Glory of God* (Christian Service Foundation, Moline, Ill.) is most helpful in answering this question: "To conclude, then, church music is good not because it is of a certain time or nationality or by a certain composer or school of musicians; nor because it is contemporary and popular; nor because it measures up to secular standards; nor just because it happens to be soft, loud, slow and steady, or fast and rhythmic. Good church music is that which does its job—reinforcing and emotionalizing the message of the words. TECHNICALLY such music will be singable and it will emphasize important words. PSYCHOLOGICALLY such music will reinforce the spirit of the words through right associations."

Values in Teaching Through Music
Music is one of the most overt learning activities emphasizing the process of "learning by doing." It is, in reality, a form of dialogue in which everyone can participate. Although some participate in greater depth in the specialization of playing instruments or singing solos, all can participate in congregational singing and the most elementary rhythmic exercises teaching simple notation and rhythmic movement in the preschool department of the Sunday School.

Most of the teaching methods discussed in this book have had rather severe restrictions with respect to age group. Teaching through music, however, is a learning approach which knows no chronological boundaries. Wayne R. Rood suggests that one of the great achievements of music is its ability to break over the age barriers and chop through the alleged generation gap.

"Meeting across these barriers is a creative achievement, educating both participants in the dialogue. Music, especially group singing, provides a bridge. It has often served that function in the past. The Moravian movement, as reported by Zinzendorf, used choirs as one of its chief educational and communal functions. Everyone in the community from youngest to oldest was in a choir of his own age. The choir was more than a musical organization in which songs were rehearsed and learned; it was also a Bible study unit, which is interesting to modern churchmen, not so much for its blending biblical theme and song, which was often bizarre, as for its achievement of togetherness" (*The Art of Teaching Christianity*, mentioned earlier).

Problems in Effective Music Education

One of the most common problems we have in music education in the church is the failure of the teacher to realize that the nature of the learner's activities, summed up in mental, intellectual, and emotional involvement, is the most important issue in method. Just as in creative art, the student should be given the opportunity to *express* himself through music even as the teacher is attempting to *impress* him with the essential message of the Gospel in song. Earl H. Gaulke suggests that we should "Listen to the rhythmic chants of childhood, and you have a key to the what and how of teaching songs. Children often express the way they feel through these half-spoken, half-sung chants, which seem to come so naturally to them" (*New Ways To Learn,* see p. 65).

Another common problem in church music education is the failure to employ and understand proper method. The teacher should stimulate and guide learning step-by-step into the opportunity for experiences not only in singing, but also listening, creating, rhythmic and instrumental participation, and music reading.

All of this may not be the responsibility of a single teacher, and it certainly does not take place in a given year of the Sunday School cycle. Nevertheless, the church needs to take a broad view of music education, recognizing that from the opening song in the nursery Sunday School worship time, to the sophisticated cantata presented by the chancel choir, it is teaching Christian music, good or bad.

A difficulty which many teachers face is that they seem to have no musical ability and yet are called upon to handle this phase of the teaching process because of the self-contained classroom. Today these teachers can draw from an arsenal of easily used helps such as record players with sing-a-long records, accompaniment tapes available in cassette or reel, and similar items to make music education possible even when there is no piano or pianist in the room. Of course it is good procedure for a Sunday School to assign a musically inclined teacher to every department so that accompaniment and music leadership needs can be taken care of properly.

Principles for Effective Music Education

Music should fit the child rather than the child fitting the music. Simple spontaneous "made-up" songs will be very appropriate and useful at the preschool level.

Utilize simplest instruments with the earliest ages to encourage participation and build interest in music. These would include sand blocks, rhythm sticks, jingle sticks, bells, triangles, tonette or flutaphone, song bells, and tambourines.

Teach the unknown by appealing to the known. Based on the child's past experience, begin with familiar songs and connect the new songs to them. This is simply an application of the old principle of apperception.

Spend time in listening activities. Let the children sit quietly while the song is sung or played, and use effective recordings in the classroom.

Be positive, encouraging, and create a joyful atmosphere at all times. There is no reason why the music time should be a forced situation to which the student looks forward with hesitation or fear.

Use effective groupings. Try to place experienced singers beside less experienced singers so that they may offer help. Teach children the harmonic structures and part singing as soon as possible.

Stress variety in your approaches to music education. Do not use a 15 minute "chorustime" in which you rehash "Everybody Ought To Know" and "God Can Do Anything" week after week. Introduce new songs in the folk style, use songbooks at times, visualize the song with printed materials or chalk drawings, and introduce hymn stories to teach the context out of which the song has arisen.

The joyful task of church music education is much more the process of listening to learn rather than learning to listen. There is an old saying expressing the virtues of song: "If music be the food of love, play on." Well, music can be the food of love — God's love in Christ. Along with our verbal teaching we can communicate the Gospel and theology in depth through the medium of music. Christian music is always music with a message.

18
Using Handwork in Church Education

"As a person learns by doing," says Katherine Tobey in *Learning and Teaching Through the Senses* (mentioned earlier), "to tie a knot, set up a tent, paddle a canoe, use a typewriter, milk a cow, he actually has to set about doing it many times in order to learn or achieve. Hearing lectures, seeing pictures, reading books, watching demonstrations, all help, but he has not learned until he himself does it."

Too often we think of handwork only as funtime or a way of keeping the children active during the times we are not teaching them. Because children have a short attention span, we vary the approaches to learning which we use in the classroom, and handwork helps to break the monotony of the hour.

But this is a very inadequate view. The Christian teacher must justify everything that he does during this teaching time, because any activity which does not lend to the accomplishing of his educational objectives is not worthy of his time. The principle of involvement can mean many things, such as intellectual, verbal, or visual participation. It can also mean tacit participation as learning takes place through use of genuinely educational handcraft procedures.

The human hand is a wonderful instrument. It is a mobile extension of the human brain and has never been satisfactorily duplicated by technology. Since the hand and brain are so closely linked in function, we ought to utilize students' hands in their learning procedures. Students may forget Bibles, manuals, and other resource materials, but they will always bring their hands to class. In the words of the Apostle Paul, "The eye cannot say unto the hand, I have no need of thee" (1 Cor. 12:21).

Values of Handwork Teaching

Interesting handwork helps a student to intelligently apply some of the concepts he has heard in class. Even when the handwork project is simple, such as connecting related numbers to form a picture of a shepherd, or coloring a picture of David and Goliath, it is a further means of input into the mind and life of that child. In this capacity, handwork serves as a support activity to learning. As a matter of fact, it would rarely be a dominant classroom procedure since by its very nature it assumes some degree of previous understanding of the subject.

Another significant factor in the use of handwork is the element of creativity which it engenders. Making something with one's hands is one of the basic elements of creativity from earliest childhood right through adulthood. It is helpful to remember then, that the wise teacher will not preempt this creativity by always specifying what kind of product he or she wants to receive from the students.

Another value of handwork teaching is the sheer pleasure which it brings to the students. To be sure, education does not exist to produce pleasure, but if fun can serve us as a means to the end of learning, then let us use it.

Problems in Using Handwork

Surely the major problem here is to avoid offering "busy work" as a part of the teaching process. Over 30 years ago James Berkeley warned us, "When the work of their hands helps the pupils form clearer mental pictures of that which they are hearing about, reading and studying, so that they understand it better, then, and then only is such activity a way of useful learning. When such work requires thinking, planning, carefulness, cooperation with others, thoughtfulness for others, service for others, it is a Christian method" (*You Can Teach*, Judson, Valley Forge, Pa.).

Another common problem is offering students handwork that is below their intellectual level. Perhaps the most common example of this is in many commercially published Junior High level Vacation Bible School curriculums. Challenged by space technology and mass media education for nine months of the year, young teens are not going to sit in a hot room during the summer and paste noodles on a board to make a plaque.

Other less significant objections sometimes raised to the use of handwork are that it is both costly and time-consuming. As a matter of fact, both of these are true to a certain extent. The investment of time in handwork makes it even more necessary that the results obtained in the process genuinely contribute to the learning experiences of the student. The cost can be overlooked by applying two general rules of education. First, it is essential to invest something if we expect to obtain satisfactory results. Second, the creative teacher will find ways and materials to make useful handwork projects available without having to spend an inordinate amount of money. Check your local bookstore for helps.

Principles for Effective Use of Handwork

As a teacher, make sure you are *not only concerned with the product, but also with the process*. The perfectionist teacher robs both herself and the children of the joy handwork can produce. She also destroys the creativity. So what if Johnny draws a church that looks like a dilapidated barn! We are not teaching art: we are teaching concepts of biblical truth.

Do not ask your students to do anything which they are physically or mentally incapable of achieving. For example, three-year-olds have trouble with scissors and could not cut out intricate patterns in a handwork project. Forcing children beyond their capability results in frustration rather than learning.

Do not force children to participate in the handwork sessions. Perhaps you can discover a reason for their reticence and reinforce whatever confidence they might have so that throughout the course of the year with you, they may learn to participate by their own choice.

Use variety in your selection of handwork projects. Do not be like the teacher who read a story for the first half hour and passed out the crayons for the second half hour every Sunday morning. The book *Creative Teaching in the Church* by Eleanor Morrison and Virgil Foster (mentioned earlier) offers a wealth of ideas for different kinds of handwork projects including the following list of creative activities for preschool children:

Play dough or clay modeling
Pasting
Stringing
Painting
Finger painting
Stamping or sponge painting
Drawing with crayons and chalk
Caring for growing things
Building with blocks

But usefulness of handwork education is not limited to preschool children. Teens and adults can profit measurably if we construct for them the kind of significant activities which deliberately leads to our learning goals.

Think through a *long-range plan* for the inclusion of handwork teaching in your classroom. If there is to be coherence in our approach to this kind of teaching, it will be brought about by our balanced approach to course planning. We dare not let handwork become a last-minute substitute for other teaching procedures.

19
The Interview
as a
Teaching Technique

We as teachers must increase the out-of-class involvement of our students. We cannot satisfactorily communicate God's truth if we are limited by existing structures to only one hour per week, and in some cases, even that rather irregularly. So we bolster our minimal classtime by trying to involve our students in learning activities during the week. The more closely we can link these outside activities to classroom methodology, the more unified the learning experience will be.

The use of interviews in class is inseparably linked to a discussion methodology. It emphasizes however, that the input for the class time can be brought to class by the students rather than the teacher. It sends the students out to deliberately confront other persons with the intent of securing information from them that will be helpful to the class.

The objective of the interview is to solicit information about a specific topic so that the class may have the opportunity of responding to this information. But there is an added dimension in using the interview: the student has the responsibility for making an approach to his informant and bringing back the information in a form that can be used for class discussion. This removes the passive element from student involvement and sends him actively into confrontation with the subject matter as well as with personalities having to do with the subject matter.

Values of Interview Teaching

One positive point has already been mentioned, the matter of participation. If we are really committed to the principle of involvement, then we will want to select teaching methodologies that will tie the students in to the entire process of teaching and learning. This is not always the case, even with some participational approaches to teaching. For example, the question and answer method is participational, but involvement only takes place at the actual classtime. This is also true of the general discussion method. But the student who interviews must be involved right from the point of assignment, through the securing of the information, to the presentation, discussion, and evaluation in the class.

Another valid plus in interview teaching is the opportunity to plug in a vast amount of information to the classroom setting. The teacher must do enough significant study so that he comes to class with a reasonable depth of knowledge. But in interviewing, the student or students will pick up different points of view and new approaches to an issue which the teacher might not have thought of while preparing the lesson largely from one point of view.

And that really suggests a third value, namely, the broad outlook on questions and issues which can suggest sources of information which have not occurred to the teacher or students up to that point. Most educators agree that a broad perspective on an issue generally results in a stronger learning experience.

Problems in Interview Teaching

To successfully utilize this classroom approach, the teacher must build genuine motivation in the students. Frequently, particularly in Sunday School settings, students are quite happy to let the teacher do the work for them. Interviewing is an attempt to delegate the responsibility for learning back to the student. At first some may be very hesitant to accept this responsibility, and the teacher will have to encourage them as well as help them carry out successful interview sessions.

Another drawback is that the student may be somewhat incompetent to formulate satisfactory interview questions. The success of the interview largely depends on the clarity and comprehensiveness of the questions used. Poor interviews then result in poor classes. Sometimes, too, it is hard to find key people who can contribute something of significance to the subject which the class is studying.

However, we too often limit interviews to so-called authorities. Surely we can get valuable points of view from ordinary people such as fellow students, friends, neighbors, adults in the church, or just the man on the street.

Perhaps the most dangerous problem of all is that the interview method may find us at classtime with nothing more than scattered human opinions on subjects of great importance. However, this only becomes a problem if we do not seriously recognize that all we sought in the first place is human opinion. It is our task in class to pour all of this information through the sieve of God's Word so that truth may come out the other end.

It is quite possible in any given class session where interview information is used that we will want to reject more of the data than we accept. This depends of course on the kind of people who were approached for the interviews. Think of the class session somewhat in the manner of the diagram on page 104.

Principles for Effective Interview Teaching

Think over a class situation in which you might want to use interviews. The controversial subject for discussion is the issue of abortion. It is your purpose in the next class session to come to grips with the question, "Should Christians defend or reject the current liberalizing trends in abortion laws and practices?" You have 12 teens in your class, and you want to send them out for interviews in the intervening week.

First of all you must *discuss the kind of people who should be interviewed.* Of course, you could send the class out "blindly," simply asking them to contact people they think would have something to contribute, but it is more effective to discuss who should be approached on the subject. There are at least four possible choices in setting up the interview structure: one student may interview one person; one student may interview several persons; multiple students may interview one person; or multiple students may interview several persons.

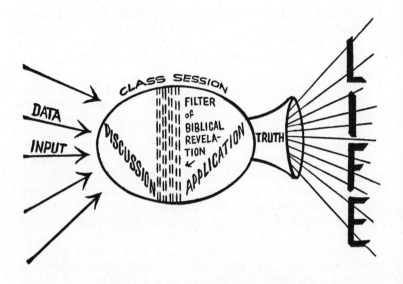

Let us assume that after your preliminary discussion, you and the class have decided to opt for plan four. Annette will approach an attorney, Sue will be interviewing the pastor, Dick will be going to the hospital to try to make contact with a doctor who has been involved in some legal abortions, and Liz wants to contact a Christian psychologist. The class and teacher then agree on the questions to be used and whether the same questions should be used for each interviewee.

The class also agrees to share the expense of Liz's contact since she will have to call the psychologist long distance and record the interview by means of a telephone hookup on her cassette recorder. Each class member will have approximately 10 minutes to present the information which he obtained so that 20 minutes of the hour can be left for open discussion.

After all of these careful plans have been laid, *share with your students some of the following basic principles of handling the interview itself.*

1. Avoid being bothersome or impertinent to the person you are contacting. Let him know right from the start that you ap-

preciate his giving his time in this way and that you will be happy to meet at his convenience and follow any "ground rules" he lays down. For example, he might want to speak so candidly that he will not want his name to be used, or he may reject the idea of recording his statements.

2. Assume the role of an inquiring reporter, but do some basic homework on the subject before you approach the interviewee. This will avoid the embarrassment of having to stop and ask definitions of terms or clarifications of ideas which could have been learned simply by doing some background reading. Incidentally, there should be essential background reading assigned to all of the class in preparation for the discussion next week.

3. Keep the interviews short. It certainly will not take long to get enough information for a 10-minute presentation. The quality of the information is not dependent upon the length of the interview, but rather the significance of the questions.

4. Do not expect the interviewee to offer an organized lecture. In fact, this is precisely what we want to avoid. If he is speaking about the subject broadly, he might avoid the questions which have been assigned and somewhat distort the specific nature of the information which we want.

5. Keep the inquiry flexible enough to take advantage of clues that arise in the course of the conversation. There might be a very strategic path that was not covered in the initial questions but which will be of great interest to the class. If the pattern of the interview is elastic, the reporter will be able to "play it by ear" in order to incorporate this key information.

As their teacher, you will want to *contact your interviewers sometime during the week* to make sure that all is proceding on schedule. Nothing could be more disastrous for next week's class than to have all four of the students turn up with no information at all. You should be available as a resource person to suggest an alternate personality if they have trouble getting in touch with the one selected.

Let me caution again that all of *the information must be subjected to the evaluative light of the Word of God.* We would certainly expect all of the persons selected in the plan above to be competent authorities on some phase of the problem of abortion.

But we should never teach the ideas of men as substitutes for the revelation of God. We will want to compare the information we get with what the Bible says about the subject of abortion. This is where you come in as the teacher. It may very well be that the pastor will offer strictly biblical information to the inquirer who approaches him. But you cannot rest on that possibility. All effective discussions must have a leader who can refer opinions and ideas to the Word of God so that they can be tested by its absolute truth.

You may also discover that the class becomes so alive and interesting that the students want to continue the discussion for another week. Try to be flexible enough in your curriculum plan to allow for expansion on a topic that has really raised what we have come to call a "teachable moment" in the life cycle of a class. Interviews may very well spark teachable moments and you will be happy that you left some of the more traditional methods behind to experiment with interviews.

20
Teaching
with Case Studies

One of my students suggested that in his view the use of case studies in teaching is merely an extension of the discussion method and not a method in itself. I believe he was at least partially right, especially if we are thinking about written case studies.

Actually the use of the case study approach can proceed at either the written or field levels. We can bring case studies into class in printed form and use them as the content of a discussion, or we can actually send our students out to do the field work of observation, analysis, and reporting on the thoughts and behavior of real, live people. Even though the second may be more difficult to activate, it seems to me that it is a very valid approach to learning.

Thinking about the use of printed cases, we should have no difficulty at all in securing the raw material. Information on the lives of people appears in newspapers, biographies, autobiographies, and frequently in fiction stories. A common prompter line in such a discussion might begin: "Say, did you read that story in this morning's newspaper about . . . ?"

Cases can also be taken out of personal experiences of either the teacher or student. Students do not have to take the role merely of analyzing cases presented to them, but may actually prepare cases individually or collectively as a group project.

The case study approach can be used to analyze a Bible character. A good example of this would be a class session devoted to an analysis of the character of Philemon and an inductive study of the book which bears his name. Obviously the provocative questions emerging from such a case study would center on the issue of slavery as well as on the role Philemon had in the Early Church.

Values of the Case Study Approach

The basic objective of the case study method is to confront the student with a real life situation. This can be achieved more easily if the subject of the study is a person confronted by the student in his own setting, but to a lesser degree it also works in the written case study. The intent is to force the application of biblical truth to a life problem. Too often we spend our time teaching propositional truth but fail to make clear-cut applications of that truth to the lives of our students.

Case study work is also usually of great interest to students. Medical schools and schools of education have popularized the approach, and management science has used it widely in the training of executive leadership. Most teachers who have experimented with it in the church have reported a high degree of enthusiasm among the students, because it provides them a reality situation against which they can measure the truth of God's Word which they are learning.

Study work is geared to teach problem-solving methods. Some Christian teachers spend classtime solving problems for their students rather than showing those students how they can solve their own problems by utilizing information in the Word of God and the creative power of the Holy Spirit in their lives. The teacher thus becomes a sort of "answering service" which the student can dial every time he has another problem or question. Such teaching fails to build initiative and independent investigation of God's truth on the part of maturing students.

When we use live case studies instead of printed ones, we take a big step forward in the development of maturity on the part of our students. Later, this chapter will illustrate one way in which live case study teaching can be used in the context of the

Sunday School. When it is used, it requires the students to involve themselves in a responsibility that will of necessity help them to mature more rapidly in a number of ways, and that is good.

Problems with Case Study Teaching

The validity of the case study approach is directly related to the reality which the cases have demonstrated. If we fail to present meaningful contemporary cases for our students to deal with, we have diminished the value of the approach. Not only that, but our students will be quick to detect the "plastic" figures we are using and will lose interest in any serious discussion of the issues.

Sometimes the discussion of a case study can degenerate into nothing more than a pooling of ignorance. That is why the group leader must be plugged in to the Word of God so that he can identify a biblical explanation and interpretation of the issues in the case.

In the use of field study cases, we might run into a problem if students are too immature. Juniors might well handle written cases in class discussion, but the use of field observation might be restricted to teens and above, or at least, to an advanced class of Junior High students.

The teacher's inability to write satisfactory cases, or even choose adequate field cases for study might also be listed as a pitfall in this method. The discussion leader is an important component part of the case study approach, but the writer of the case study is even more strategic.

Principles for Effective Case Study Teaching

Sometimes it takes a while to come to grips with the crucial issues in the analysis of a case study. This can be true of written cases, but it is certainly true of field study cases. We might say that the first principle is *do not rush the study*. Martha Leypoldt suggests that in the process of analysis and problem solving, so essential in case study work, there are nine "relevant facts" which must be gathered by students (*40 Ways to Teach in Groups,* mentioned earlier):

1. The people involved
2. The historical background of the situation
3. The relationships among persons or groups involved

4. The religious background and perspective of the situation
5. The sociological factors involved
6. The economic factors involved
7. The educational backgrounds of persons involved
8. The ethnic origins of the persons involved
9. The tensions causing the problem

Another principle is to encourage our classes to concentrate on *learning to share their points of view.* To put it another way, students ought to be learning from each other's cases as well as from cases they are studying directly. In the discussion of each case there will doubtless be insights and ideas offered by other class members which will help the person who is handling it to deal with it more effectively and thoroughly.

A third principle in the use of case studies is the necessity for trying to *formulate specific solutions and analysis* once the real problems have been identified. Stay away from muddy thinking or rash commitments and avoid criticism of the person in the case, particularly in field research and the study of living personalities. A constant question to be asked in the analysis and discussion of case studies begins with the word *why?*

How can field study analysis be used in the context of a Sunday School class? Meet Jack Thorpe, a teen student (a high school junior) in a Sunday School class at an evangelical church. His class has been discussing the relationship of the Jews and the Samaritans, and he has learned something of the historical background — how these people were forced to live together after the postexilic return of the Jews.

This discussion gave birth to a comparison of Samaritan problems with the relationship of majority and minority groups in Jack's own city. Obviously there are some features of Jewish-Samaritan relations which did not fit, but Jack's teacher urges each student to select a young member of a minority group in the city and try to learn everything about that person that can be learned within a month. One month after the original assignment, the class will begin analyzing their findings, taking the next month or two to discuss the kind of ministry their church can have to members of minority groups.

Jack selects Manuel Lopez, a young Chicano boy, who lives down the block from the church. Though Jack's church is adjacent to the Mexican-American community, Manuel knows very little about the church except that it is a building on a certain corner in his neighborhood. Within the next month Jack will spend as much time as he can with Manuel. He will go to his home. He will visit his school. He will spend time with him discussing how he feels about life, his family, his school, and what the future might hold for him. Jack will interview his parents and perhaps some of his friends. He may even ask Manuel to write a brief biography describing how he sees himself as a resident of the Mexican community in the city.

Along the way Jack will attempt to share the Gospel without being "pushy" or impolite. He realizes that Manuel is graciously allowing him to study something very private, his own life, and wants to win his confidence and friendship during this period of the study.

Other students in Jack's class will be doing the same thing with members of the Negro community, the Chinese community, and other minority groups in the city. Their purpose, besides sharing their faith with these other young people, is to put together a report on how their church can minister to minority groups within the city while still keeping its theological and denominational distinctions. To put it another way, what can the church do and what can Jack's Sunday School class do to win boys and girls like Manuel to Christ and help them grow to be disciples of the Lord Jesus?

Difficult? Yes, to be sure. But also practical and very interesting for students. Now the class is *theirs!* Now they are involved in the teaching-learning process! How much better this is than just having an imaginary case study prepared by the teacher for purposes of discussion in the class. It will take creativity, and perhaps in your church, a healthy measure of courage. But it can be done. And it certainly is worthy of your consideration as a creative and progressive teacher of the Word of God.

21
Drama
in the Classroom

Some have suggested that drama teaches us about life in a way that is clearer and more vivid that we normally live it. It tends to sort out complex problems in human lives, not by simplification, but through selection. Drama can make stories and ideas come alive, and, because of its vital and creative nature, it is often a significant educational technique.

When we are thinking about the educational context of church and Sunday School, we are thinking almost exclusively about "religious drama" and more specifically "Christian drama." Kaye Baxter defines religious drama as dealing with significant and vital themes of life. It "presents characters in action — in situations where faith and belief are tested" (*Contemporary Theater and the Christian Faith,* Abingdon, Nashville, Tenn.).

Remember we are thinking here about effective methods for the communication of an absolute message. One must not be swayed by the fallacious argument of guilt by association and thereby conclude that because drama and theater have been improperly used to convey error and sin, the method is corrupt and ought to be avoided. Drama as a technique is amoral; it has no inherent characteristics of good or evil in itself. How we use it makes the difference.

The Old Testament provides ample precedent for this kind of teaching. Consider the prophet Ezekiel designing a model of the city of Jerusalem and then laying siege to it at the command of Jehovah. Or the behavior of Elijah on Mount Carmel as recorded in 1 Kings 18. It was not necessary to call for all those extra buckets of water or to taunt the prophets of Baal about the vacation patterns of their gods. But all of this added to the climactic moment when Elijah drove home the point of the exclusive power of the God of the Bible. Dramatic demonstrations on the part of the prophets were a basic format of instruction during those days.

We should not confuse drama with role playing, which as presented in an earlier chapter, can be utilized in less than a half hour period with virtually no preparation on the part of the participants. Such is rarely the case with drama. Here we are talking about a method we might employ only once or twice a year. The long rehearsals, costuming, stage layout, and other preparations tend to make us think that drama as a teaching method is really "not worth it." But we should not be too hasty to condemn any teaching methodology — at least until we have tried it. The impact which effective drama can have on the lives of the participants as well as the audience may be well worth the time invested.

Values in the Use of Drama

Drama can be very effective in pinpointing solutions to problems which people face in real life. Emotional involvement is a common experience when one is viewing an effective play. He may see himself reflected in one of the characters and recognize that the same solutions explored in the play are applicable to his own life and problems.

Drama can also be used to enhance worship experiences. James Warren reminds us, "Drama has always been closely related to the worship of the church. For example, interpretive reading, chorus speech, artful pageantry, dramatic movement, tasteful decor, and imaginative lighting are but a few techniques that can bring a congregation into a mood of worship. Drama is not only to be found in these recognizable techniques, but it can be discovered as an impetus in liturgical worship (i.e. when a service of worship steadily progresses toward movements of adoration and commitment)" ("Art in the Church," *Religious Education,* Marvin J. Taylor, ed., Abingdon, Nashville, Tenn.).

I shall never forget an experience I had at a Good Friday service some years ago. Instead of the usual choral selections and sermons, the church utilized a film on the Crucifixion. The impact of that drama upon my life at that point was far more significant than many other services attended in previous years.

Another helpful feature of drama is its ability to stimulate thought on significant issues. In this way, drama could be used as a catalyst to group discussion. Used in such a manner, we would probably avoid many of the problems of costuming and rehearsal since we would want such a drama to be short enough in production that effective use of discussion time could immediately follow its presentation.

For example, a Junior High class studying Paul's missionary journeys in the Book of Acts might prepare a dramatic presentation of the experience of Paul and Silas in the Philippian jail. Two or three rehearsals with very limited use of costuming ought to yield a profitable presentation of 15 or 20 minutes length which could then be followed by total group discussion.

Drama can help reveal insights into the character and personality of persons portrayed in the play. Think of the impact of a carefully planned and executed play probing the attitudes of Job during his time of suffering.

Drama can aid the church in evangelism. Non-Christian parents who might never come to a regular service of the church might be enthusiastically responsive to an invitation asking them to come and see a play in which one or more of their children is acting. The impact of the message of the play could be aimed at a clear presentation of the Gospel. The wide acceptance of the Billy Graham Evangelistic Association film ministry is sufficient justification for the role of drama in evangelism.

If the church ever uses television on a large scale, it may very well discover (as some major denominations have already shown us in their television work) that Christian drama is a more effective technique in the communication of the Gospel through television than more traditional approaches.

One further point should be made with respect to the use of creative drama with children. Eleanor Morrison and Virgil Foster devote a chapter to this and point out how drama can be effective even without long rehearsals and expensive costuming. "Creative drama is a favorite activity of children because they make up their own dramatization. The material may be original or it may be based on a story that the group is studying. There is little or no scenery, costuming, or properties. The dialogue, because it grows out of immediate interaction, varies with each repetition. Emphasis is on free and spontaneous participation by as many children as possible rather than on acting excellence. The cast may be changed each time that a scene is played, for all the children should be involved" (*Creative Teaching in the Church,* mentioned earlier).

Problems in Using Drama

In attempting to make a case for using drama, I have already mentioned most of the potential problems. Surely our hesitancy in using the method is based on the negative associations we have concerning theater in general. Add to that the horrifying prospect of weeks or months of rehearsals, accompanied by the expense of costuming and staging, and the combination is enough to drive any teacher back to the lecture method!

One of my students, writing a paper on the use of drama, suggested a pattern for introducing drama as a teaching technique in the church. He listed eight steps which should be taken as a group can handle them.

1. Lecture — the present status of many classes
2. Discussion — a first step into involvement procedures
3. Discussion of how a character thinks, or how a person should react to what was discussed
4. Discussion of religious plays and how they may help explain situations in the Christian life
5. Role playing — the dimension at which participants take on a certain characteristic and act it out with others
6. Improvisations — short original sketches portraying some idea or mimicking some personage
7. Short scenes — introduce scripts and maybe begin to think in terms of costuming
8. One-act plays — fully scripted and with rehearsals before the drama is played to an audience

The result of these eight steps would culminate in full length plays and the use of drama as a regular medium in the church's education program.

Principles for the Effective Use of Drama

Be patient with participants who have not had experience; patient with adults in the church who are a bit leery of the method; patient in seeing the results of drama as a teaching technique.

If you anticipate using drama outside your own classroom or group, *check with all necessary authorities* in the church to make sure you have full clearance for developing the play.

Exercise great care in the *choice of the play.* Make sure it is not too difficult for the age group and that its essential message conveys precisely what you intend to achieve in meeting the objectives of the teaching situation.

Choose a director who can competently guide the development of the play. If you are to be the director yourself, study some helpful resource books to enhance the effectiveness of your leadership. Here are a few suggestions:

Drama In The Church, Fred Eastman, Samuel French Inc., New York, N.Y.

Religious Drama — Its Means and Ends, Harold Ehrensberger, Abingdon, Nashville, Tenn.

Stage Scenery and Lighting: A Handbook for Nonprofessionals, Samuel Selden and Hulton D. Sallman, Appleton-Century-Crofts, New York, N.Y.

22
Creative Writing as a Teaching Technique

When my wife was the superintendent of the Junior Department in our Sunday School, she asked her Juniors in the 15-minute worshiptime to write a paragraph describing their understanding of what God is like. Here are a few samples of the results:

"Well, I think He is a bearded man with long hair, brown, loving eyes, and raggedy clothing."

"God is a great man. God is joy and happiness. He is tall and kind. He is a great man-shaped light sitting on a throne in a cloud."

"God is a nice person who has feelings. I think God looks like the pictures they show. God probably looks somewhat like we do because it says in Genesis that we were created in His image. He must be very beautiful with soft curly hair. He's real happy up there. He laughs too because it says so in the Bible 'He that sitteth in heaven laughs' (or something like that)."

Think of the value of these expressions to both the students and the teachers in that Junior Department! The students are forced to verbalize their ideas about God and thereby get some idea of how developed or undeveloped those concepts might be. The teachers gain insight into the theological needs of their students and what specific misconceptions about God need to be broken down before the inculcation of biblical theology can gain a solid foothold.

Of course, creative writing as a teaching technique covers a great many more activities than just a descriptive paragraph in the Junior Department. It does not have to take place with the pencil in the student's hand. In the earliest years of the Preschool Departments, children can talk about their experiences and reactions to pictures as a teacher writes down some of the responses and later reads them back to the children.

Older children may work on diaries, record books, stories, rhymes and poems, descriptions of pictures, and writing plays.

Teens and adults can participate in creative writing by developing poems and stories which illustrate certain biblical truths being studied in class.

Values of Creative Writing

Perhaps the most significant value of creative writing is the exploration into self which it provides. When we articulate our feelings or ideas about a certain matter on paper, we tend to discipline our minds into orderly thinking about that subject. That is why college teachers so frequently assign term papers and other writing projects which call for the discipline of organized thought process.

Actually we have already pinpointed three values: insight into self, discipline, and organization of one's thinking.

Wright Pillow suggests that transposing a Bible story or finishing an open-ended life situation story both help the writer to find in the experience of his subject some solutions which are helpful to him. "The usefulness of this kind of experience becomes even more apparent when we evaluate it in terms of 'learning at the intersection.' Visualize two streets coming together at an intersection. One of the streets we can label 'The Gospel,' that which is true and unchanging. The other we can label 'Life Situation,' that which must change constantly. Where these two intersect, Christian education can take place. When the Gospel is allowed to clarify and redirect the life situation of an individual, a new person is born" (*Creative Procedures for Adult Groups,* Harold D. Minor, ed., Abingdon, Nashville, Tenn.).

Creative writing is sometimes used as an effective response to some other kind of methodology such as a sermon, lecture, or discussion. Phyllis W. Sapp includes the following example of a poem written by a 13-year-old boy after listening to a sermon on the transfiguration of Christ ("What is Death?" *Creative Teaching in the Church School,* Broadman, Nashville, Tenn.).

What is Death?

Death. What is Death?
To an atheist but an end,
A trip out of life and to the end.
People cry over this one,
For they think he's gone forever.

Death. What is Death?
To a non-Christian, a terror.
A trip out of life to hell,
And he knows it,
A desperate call for a minister,
And then slipping off in a terror.

Death. What is Death?
To Christians but a joyful end,
From an earthly trek to see their Lord.
They slip away in happiness,
For they see their Lord coming for them.
There is no sadness in their home.
For by and by they shall meet again.

Problems in Creative Writing

Some teachers do not use creative writing simply because they think it is a waste of time. After all, is not our job as Christian teachers to inculcate the concrete propositions of objective truth? How can we justify allowing students to pour out their own un-developed ideas when they should be filling their minds with the kind of biblical information which only the teacher can provide?

No doubt creative writing (like any other method) *could* be-come a waste of time. The unskilled teacher attempting to preside over an undisciplined class, would almost certainly be guilty of wasting time regardless of what method he chose. We must understand that methodology is merely a vehicle or transportation device by which we want to convey propositional truth to students. The very fact that the student takes into consideration as he is writing what the Bible says about his subject is a good step toward helping him to make application of important truths to his life.

It is not our purpose merely to parrot truth into the air. As teachers we want to see that truth takes root in the lives of our students and, in turn, brings forth fruit in the behavior of those students. Wright Pillow suggests that "creative writing has endless possibilities for making the 'Gospel learned about' into the 'Gospel acted out.' The writer's reactions when he sees his thoughts on paper may even create a desired change."

Like any other method, creative writing should not be overused. It is an excellent supplement to other methods and therefore can render an effective supporting role.

Principles for Effective Use of Creative Writing

Make sure the writing project has a clear-cut *learning objective*. It is not just time filler nor an attempt to secure physical participation in the classtime. The objective of the paragraph about God was to get students to think honestly about what they understood God to be like (no child signed his paper). Perhaps our goal will be worship or analysis of a given passage by asking for an interpretive paraphrase. Whatever the objective, we should be clear in our minds as teachers so that we can communicate proper direction in giving the writing assignment.

Use variety in creative writing. How about writing a newspaper or developing an entire worship service with songs and themes? Teen-agers could write a radio script or a narrative for a slide presentation. How about writing a choral reading, psalm, folk song, or doctrinal statement? The possibilities are almost endless.

Do not get hung up on style or grammatical excellence. The main purpose of creative writing is content. No doubt there is some virtue in disciplining students to write everything in proper form, but such an inhibition might stifle the kind of creativity we want in an honest *reflection of student attitude*.

If you begin to use creative writing on a fairly extensive scale, hold on to the masterpieces you get from your students. Perhaps some day you will be able to publish a best-seller, or at least contribute a column on creative writing to a Christian periodical.

23
Developing
Instructive Assignments

Twelve-year-old Marty does not like Sunday School. He comes, but only because his parents force him. And his attitude clearly shows all the while he is in class that he does not really want to be there. Occasionally he gets excited about a Christmas party or a contest of some kind. But the general week-by-week activities hold no interest for him. From all outward appearances, he is learning very little about the Bible and the Christian faith. One thing is sure. Whatever exposure Marty has to eternal truth comes exclusively in the one hour on Sunday morning because *he does not spend five minutes in God's Word during the week!*

The great tragedy is that Marty is only too typical of countless young people in many evangelical Sunday Schools across the nation. His parents are Christians, which means to them that they attend Sunday School and church on Sunday morning but somehow does not seem to include any responsibility for Christian nurture of their son at home. Their interest in Sunday School however, seems to be sincere, and they are very careful to ensure Marty's attendance week by week.

A wise teacher could do something about this difficult situation. No doubt visitation and a counseling ministry with the parents would be a positive step. Short of that, a teacher who really became serious about his students' responsibility to study at home could develop assignments which would double or even triple Marty's exposure to the Word of God.

The wise teacher will remember too, that it is the parents' responsibility to make sure work outside of the classroom gets done, and he would enlist the support of Marty's mom and dad right from the beginning. He would find allies in Marty's parents for they would help the boy with the assignments and at least provide some leverage at home to see that the work was completed each week.

Values of Assignments

One value should be already obvious. If Marty's parents are helping him with his assignments, they are also being exposed to God's Word and that Junior High teacher is having a ministry to parents as well as to his student. But effective securing of parental support depends upon whether the Sunday School teacher has really accepted the premise that he alone cannot handle the task of Christian nurture. Findley Edge makes it very plain when he says, *"The church cannot accomplish the task of religious education alone.* That may seem like a shocking and extreme statement to some; nevertheless, it is true. The sooner church leaders and parents face this fact the better it will be" (*Helping The Teacher,* mentioned earlier).

The use of assignments also puts "more school in Sunday School." It raises the academic level of church education, and, even though you might have difficulties in getting your students enthused about "doing homework" at first, a careful system of reinforcement coupled with parental support can and will win the battle. As mentioned above, a carefully planned assignment program can double or triple the classtime, and every Sunday School teacher ought to be excited about it for that reason if for no other.

One of the most significant values of assignments however, is their ability to relate to life outside of the unreal situation which we call "class." This implies that the assignment is more than just filling in the blanks or memorizing the names of the books of the Bible. If we can design "life-related assignments," we can assist the student in putting into practice those things which he has learned in class.

Finally, we ought to use assignments because of their capacity to stimulate inquiry which might result in spiritual growth. If we really believe in the supernatural power of the Word of God, then we must believe that the more time a student genuinely spends in studying the Word of God the more spiritual growth will result. A spirit of inquiry will also lead to teachable moments in the classtime as the student raises questions or problems which he has encountered in the work he attempted to do at home.

Problems in Using Assignments

Perhaps the most common problem we face in attempting to get Sunday School students to work at home is the problem of negative attitudes. Somehow the idea of homework seems to correlate well with schooling during the week. But we have portrayed the image that Sunday School should be easy and not have any effort connected with it. It is hard to shake an image, particularly when it is a bad one. But this is one we will simply have to lose if we are going to minister God's Word effectively at acceptable levels of education in the evangelical church. We may have to start out slowly with simple assignments and try to make them as interesting as possible, but we should get serious about the importance of assignments as a method.

Time is always a problem. The students are busy, and the activities of school and community tend to crowd out the time necessary to "work on the Sunday School lesson." That is why good teachers will make occasional telephone calls during the week to offer assistance with the assignment or even to build in some kind of reward system. A teacher I know has a standard procedure whereby he calls one member of his class each week, but no one knows in advance who will be called. If the selected student has done his lesson by the time of the call (usually Thursday or Friday evening) he gets 10 bonus points in the current class contest.

Another common difficulty is that some printed curriculum materials do not offer challenging and attractive assignments. Sometimes the level is below the students for whom it was written, and sometimes it is too difficult. It is possible to have both of these problems with the same material in the same class because of varying backgrounds of the students.

This is where the teacher comes in. He can add to or vary the regular curriculum plan because he alone knows the specific needs and problems of his own class. Let us by all means use the best curriculum materials we can buy, but *let us* never give up by default our right as classroom teachers to determine what is best for our particular students.

Principles for Effective Use of Assignments

Involve the students in selecting the assignment initially. This is simply the process of adopting a positive use of peer pressure. Rather than handing down the assignment each week, let the students talk in class about what kind of carry-over activities would be meaningful and interesting to them. A worker is always more thorough in following through on a plan, if he has had a significant role in making it.

Make the assignments life-related. Get away from the traditional "knowledge storehouse" kind of study, and have your students touch life in the context of the subject matter. Some of the earlier chapters discuss the methods which would adapt themselves well to life-related assignments (for example, using interviews in your teaching).

Always check the assignment after it has been given. The old adage reminds us that "the worker does what the boss inspects and not what he expects." This will take time, but if we are going to commit ourselves to a methodology which includes assignments, we are going to have to accept the responsibility for checking the work. Nothing will kill the progress of achievement faster than ignoring the work that a student has done in preparation for his Sunday School class.

Use good principles of motivation. There are a number of ways to *build motivation* in students and most of them are perfectly acceptable. The idea of peer group involvement was mentioned above. Competition is an extrinsic motivator, but at certain age levels it can be used very positively. Ultimately we want to build intrinsic motivation, which causes the student to study God's Word because he knows it is important for him to do so.

Vary the types of assignments. Use reading and research, interviews, prepared questions, projects, observation work, reports, preparation of panels and debates, and any other approach which will lead the student into the Word during the week. Obviously, assignments can be coupled with other kinds of teaching methodology to make an interesting and effective class.

Reinforce all efforts the student makes to work outside of class. Reinforcement can take the form of verbal commendation or extrinsic rewards such as stars on a chart which will ultimately culminate in winning some kind of competition.

But, let me say it one more time — all of this work is futile unless the teacher deliberately, carefully, and thoroughly involves the parents in overseeing, helping, and expediting the work at home. In the final analysis, Christian nurture is the task of the parents, and the Sunday School teacher is only a supporting and assisting worker. We must help parents see this responsibility and act positively upon it.

24
Testing
as a
Teaching Method

In a very real sense testing evaluation is always going on. But it does not always take the form of a teaching method. Sometimes tests are used as evaluation instruments (that's good). Sometimes they are used as a threat (that's bad). Rarely are they used as a means to convey truth (that's unfortunate).

There are a number of ways that students' learning can be tested. Almost all of them are adaptable for use as a teaching method. The way we use a test makes it a teaching tool, so we can get double mileage out of any given evaluation instrument simply by adapting it for both evaluation and teaching.

Here are some types of testing which are commonly used in most levels of education and certainly would be very usable in church education as well:

Matching Questions. On this kind of test the student links up the items in one column which go correctly with the items in another column.

(SAMPLE)

a. David   1. Was taken captive to Babylon _____
b. Daniel   2. Ministered to the Jews in exile _____
c. Jonah   3. Was the youngest son of Jesse _____
d. Ezekiel   4. Preached a revival in Nineveh _____

True-False Test. This is perhaps the easiest to construct and the quickest to administer. Its major weakness lies in the temptation to use trick questions (never a good procedure if we want the test to be a teaching tool), and the fact that a student has a 50 percent chance of getting the answer right even if he never studied the material at all.
(SAMPLE)
Mark T or F after the following sentences to indicate whether they are true or false.
1. Jesus was born in Nazareth. _____
2. Jesus baptized many disciples Himself. _____
3. Jesus cast the beggars out of the Temple. _____

Completion Tests. In the completion test the student fills in the information indicated in a blank space or spaces.
(SAMPLE)
The name of Abraham's wife was _____, and the name of his favorite son was _____.

Multiple Choice Tests. A multiple choice test is one in which the student reads a question and then selects his answer from a list of alternatives (usually four) which are provided for him.
(SAMPLE)
When God confronted him in a bright light, Saul of Tarsus was on his way to what city? _____
a. Jerusalem
b. Damascus
c. Babylon
d. Rome

In one of my books I have indicated four guidelines for the use of multiple choice questions.
1. Avoid listing obviously wrong alternatives
2. Make sure that one of the alternatives is distinctly better than the others
3. Place all of the essential information in the question
4. Be sure that each of the alternatives grammatically fits into the sentence

(*Understanding Teaching,* ETTA, Wheaton, Ill.).

Essay Questions. This kind of test takes more time because a student must respond to the questions by writing the answer in his own words. Although it takes more time to grade and more time to complete, the value of having the student verbalize truth is a desirable gain.

(SAMPLE)

Write three or four sentences describing what the Bible says about Christ's coming again (you may use your Bible in answering the question).

Values of Testing as a Teaching Method

A teacher who accepts the responsibility to teach also accepts the responsibility to evaluate learning. Paul Lederach suggests four areas of evaluation which are important in Christian teaching:

1. We can test persons in the area of knowledge and understanding.
2. We can evaluate habits that contribute to a Christian personality such as prayer, Bible study, honesty, self-control, and loyalty.
3. We can evaluate changes in values and attitudes.
4. We can evaluate a person's participation in the gathered life of the church and his participation in the mission of the church as a witness and servant when the church is scattered (*Learning To Teach,* mentioned earlier).

Stimulation is another value of testing. Sometimes I will give a complete test the first day a class convenes. The purpose is to show students what they know *and what they do not know* about that particular subject. Hopefully, this awareness motivates learning.

The teacher who tests his students regularly can be a source of information on the progress those students are making in the Christian life.

Problems in Using Testing

Just as in making assignments, the biggest problem we face in testing is the problem of poor attitudes. It is not easy to "sell" the idea of the importance of testing. This is a problem faced in all education even though no serious educator would discount the importance of evaluation of some kind. Lederach quotes the old guideline, "We test our teaching to be sure we know what we are doing and are doing what we know!"

Sometimes testing becomes a problem because we have poor test instruments. Fortunately, most of the major curriculum publishers are now producing standardized Bible knowledge tests to coordinate with the curriculum at most age levels. Please remember, though, that these are strictly content-knowledge tests and do not measure attitudes and behavioral change. These things must be evaluated by subjective observation over a period of time.

Principles for Effective Testing

Test for more than memorization. Although Bible knowledge is a basic area, the teacher should also try to test attitudes, choices, and conduct.

Always *build your test on the basis of your teaching-learning objectives.* If you have clearly stated objectives at the beginning of a quarter and also before each week, you will have some basis upon which to develop a test. It is foolish to try to test students to see if they know what you never specifically set out to teach them in the first place.

Always *explain the test content and procedure* carefully. Let the student know precisely what is expected of him, how he should prepare for the test, and what kinds of things he should do in writing the test.

Try to *remove the element of threat* as much as possible. In the early days you may forego the collecting of papers and let the test be a personal experience of the student's measurement of his own progress. Above all, never use a test as a form of punishment.

Involve the parents. Remember that theme? Let the parents know when a test is scheduled so they can help at home in the preparation and study.

Make good tests. You may not have access to standardized tests provided by a publisher. Or, you may for some reason choose not to use them or supplement the standardized test by tests which you make yourself. In preparing a teacher-made test try to observe the following positive characteristics:

1. Objectivity — try to develop tests which have specific kinds of information feedback even when that information is of an understanding or comprehension type rather than fact memorization.

2. Clarity — questions should not be vague or capable of more than one correct interpretation.
3. Comprehensiveness — a test is comprehensive when it touches on each of the major areas of the unit studied.
4. Validity — test what is supposed to be tested. If we intend our tests to measure a student's understanding of what salvation is, the test is invalid if we only get back a series of memorized facts which may not tell us anything about how well he understands the process of conversion.

If testing is really to become a teaching technique, we should take one further step after the test has been taken and graded. We should *bring it back into class and discuss it thoroughly* with our students so they may have on opportunity to see where they made mistakes and what kinds of things will be necessary for further study.